# The History of Fiji

Alfred G. Mayer

# The History of Fiji

LM Publishers

# PART I

Of all the island groups in the outer Pacific none surpass the Fijis in their rare combination of beautiful scenery and interesting natives. The islands are upon the opposite side of the world from England, for the meridian of 180° passes through the centre of the group crossing the island of Taviuni. The islands lie from 15° 30' to 19° 30' south of the equator, and are thus south of the region of perpetual trade winds, but still well within the tropics, the center of the group being about 1,000 miles due north from New Zealand.

That dauntless old rover, Abel Jansen Tasman, discovered them in 1643 on his way from Tonga in the *Heemskirk* and *Zeehaan* and named them "Prince William's Islands" and "Heemskirk's Shoals." After this, they were all but forgotten until July 2, 1774, when Captain James Cook sighted the small island of Vatoa in the extreme southeastern end of the group. The natives fled into the forest upon the approach of his boat, and he contented himself by leaving a knife, some medals and nails in a conspicuous place. Finding many sea-turtles in the region, he named his land-fall "Turtle Island," and then departed from the Fijis never to return.

In May, 1789, Captain Bligh sailed through the group in the small open boat in which he made the voyage of 3,600 miles from Tonga to Timor, this feat being celebrated in Byrons's poem "The Island." He was pursued by two canoes from Waya Island, and dared not land nor hold any communication with the natives. Later in 1792, Bligh again sailed among the Fijis, this time while in command of the man-of-war *Providence,* and in 1796 Captain Wilson cruised among the islands upon his missionary voyage in the *Duff.* Thus gradually the group became known to Europeans; but remained uncharted until 1840, when the United States Exploring Expedition, under Wilkes, made a survey of the region. Indeed, the oldest detailed accounts of the islands and their inhabitants is that given by Wilkes in the third volume of his narrative of the expediton.

Counting isolated rocks, the archipelago is composed of about 270 islands having a total area of 7,400 square miles, or nearly the same as that of Massachusetts. Two of the islands are far larger than the others, Vanua Levu (the great island) being about 100 miles long and 25 miles wide. and Viti Levu (Great Viti) being 80 miles long and 55 wide. Kandavu and Taviuni have not one twentieth the land area of the two larger islands, and all the others are much smaller, so small indeed that only about 80 islands of the group are large enough to be inhabited.

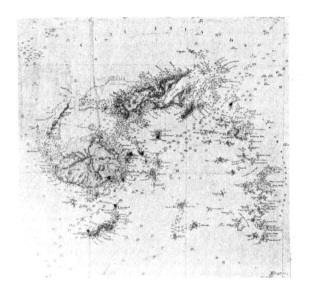

Geologically speaking, the Fijis are old and the volcanoes which gave rise to them have long ago subsided into their final rest. Yet even to-day there are reminders of more active times in an occasional earthquake, or the hot springs of Ngau or of Savu Savu valley and other places on Vanua Levu, or the pumice, which at times rises to the surface of the sea and is cast ashore at Kandavu. The islands were once much larger and higher than they are to-day, for tropical rains have washed the soft lavas into the surrounding sea, leaving here and there pinnacles of hard basalt towering upward in fantastic castellated forms and imparting a romantic beauty to the view which is surpassed only in the Society and Marquesas Islands. The little island of Kobu near Nairai is a mass of volcanic rock, 90 feet in height, and is so strongly magnetic that a compass placed upon its summit is deflected 85°.

In the Fijis the erosion has gone so far that most of the old volcanic rims have disappeared. Totoya and Thombia are, however, beautiful cup-like craters, their centers now being harbors encircled by crescent shaped ridges, and there are a few fairly M-ell-defined craters among the mountains of the larger islands. Indeed, at Kambara a small volcano has in recent, but still prehistoric, times broken through the elevated coral reef, but no native myths speak of volcanic eruptions.

The Fijis are much older than the large islands of the Hawaiian group or than some of the Samoan and Tongan islands, the volcanoes of which are still active. Indeed, in the interior of Viti Levu plutonic rocks and slates are found attesting to the considerable age of this island, allying it to such land masses as New Zealand or New Caledonia, which are partly volcanic and partly continental in character. Thus the Fijis differ from the simple volcanic tumuli which constitute the Hawaiian, Samoan, Society and Marquesas islands. In Hawaii and Tahiti we find great central volcanic peaks, from the summits of which deep valleys radiate outward to the sea, but in Fiji the large islands have been formed by fusions between many adjacent volcanic cones, and in later times the erosion has gone so far and local elevations and depressions have been so frequent that the landscape is broken and wholly irregular.

Indeed, the islands have not been passive during all the ages in which the rains have worn them down, for there have been depressions and also great upheavals here and there, as at Yanua Mbalavu, where the old coral reef is now a bold precipice of overhanging castellated craffs towering far above the waves that dash at its feet. This old coral rock is cavernated and, at least one place along the shore, at Black Swan Point, on Yanua Mblavu Island, one may enter through a small cleft in the precipice and find oneself in a spacious chamber several hundred feet in height, with veil-like sheets of stalactites sparkling in the dim light that wanders inward through some hidden rift far up in the vaulted roof. A deep pool of wonderfully clear ocean water lies within this shadowy retreat, and brilliant blue and green fish flit butterfly-like through their natural aquarium, the floor of which is carpeted by graceful sea-whips, and slowly creeping crinoids with long feathery arms.

Many other islands also exhibit elevated coral reefs, which in some cases, as at Vatu Vara, have been lifted nearly 1,000 feet above the sea, and, near Suva, the hillside is full of fossil sea-shells and corals. We can see that the islands were once much larger than they are to-day, for nearly everyone is encircled by a coral reef several miles out to sea, which marks the contour of the old coast line. Indeed, at Astrolabe Reef, we find a small cavernated volcanic rock, the last remnant of an island, surrounded by a broad lagoon which is edged on its seaward side by a rim of coral reef over which the surf breaks ceaselessly. In other cases, as at Cakau-momo, the island has washed away and only the submerged reef is left to mark its former site.

*A Ravine in Fiji, Viti Levu Island.*

The very land has age and life and is vanishing before our eyes. In the past the islands were higher, but now the loftiest mountain peaks are not over 4,600 feet.

The earthquake waves, which must have accompanied many of the changes of elevation, may have given rise to the myth of a deluge, which under varied forms is found almost universally among the natives of the tropical Pacific, but we need not resort to such remote or hypothetical occasions for the establishment of the flood-myths, for almost every year between February and March there is a severe storm in Fiji, and recent floods of the Rewa River are now the topic of native song.

It is to the rich tropical forest which clothes them that the Fijis owe their charm. Even the sheltered relatively dry leeward slopes of the mountains are fairly well covered with forest, but on the sides which face the southeast trade wind the vegetation crowds into every nook and cranny of the precipices even to the summits of the highest peaks. So copious is the rainfall that the Rewa River is larger than any in England and is navigable for fifty miles above its mouth, its width being fully three thousand yards, where it meets the ocean.

The beauty of the mountain valleys produces an impression which time cannot efface from the memory. Great Tahitian chestnuts, the "Ivi" (*Inocarpus edulis*), with buttressed trunks, tower far above like columns of an ancient temple garlanded in green, while overarching the rock pools of the stream are the rich brown stems of tree-ferns crowned by emerald sprays of nature's lace-work. Broad-leaved caladiums cluster in the water, and the clambering Pandanus winds in reptilian folds over the high boughs, where dainty orchids nestle far from the reach of all below. Now and again there is a flash of color, where some cockatoo or parrot or brilliant butterfly appears only to vanish in the leafy maze, or here and there through a break in the canopy a furtive beam of sunlight penetrates to gild the greenness of the shade. One looks in vain for dead trees and old decaying logs for all is life in this luxuriant growth. Death has here no lasting place, for termites and ants and a host of parasitic plants set hungrily upon all that weaken, and the dying trunk shrinks into other greenness and passes phoenix-like into other life. Wilkes spoke truly when he said of the islands, "So beautiful was their aspect that I could scarcely bring my mind to the realizing sense of the well-known fact that they were the abode of a savage, ferocious and treacherous race of cannibals." Today there are no cannibals, and one is safer in "dark Fijia" than in the streets of any civilized city.

*Canoes at Kambara Island, Fiji.*

An extraordinary number of the forest trees of the Fijis furnish food for man. Such are the breadfruit, which grows to be 50 feet high, with deeply incised glossy leaves, sometimes almost two feet long. The Malay apple, or kavika (*Eugenia*), grows to a great height and bears a delicious fruit, which, when ripe, is white, streaked with delicate pink, and most refreshing and rose-like to the taste. The cocoanut palm clusters in dense groves along the beaches, the long leaves murmuring to the sea breeze as they wave to and fro, casting their grateful shade upon the native village. Of all trees none is more useful to tropical man than the cocoanut. In time of drought it provides a life sustaining drink, its leaves serve to thatch the sides of houses and its nuts become drinking cups, or provide oil or food; its wood serves for manifold purposes; its terminal bud is the celery of the tropical epicurean, and the sap from its flower-stalk provides an intoxicating beverage. Indeed, to do justice to its uses would lead us so far afield that we must perforce desist. Curiously, the cocoanut thrives only on the lowlands near the ocean, and flourishes best where the sea-spray settles upon its leaves, or even where its roots sink beneath the level of the salt water. Very rarely one sees a cocoanut palm growing upon the mountain side at Tahiti, up to 800 feet above the sea, but this is exceptional. Bananas and the wild plantain (Fei) grow luxuriantly in the forest, as do also oranges, lemons, limes, shaddocks, guavas, alligator pears, the papaw, mango and many other smaller shrubs and vegetables. Indeed, from remote times the natives have cultivated the soil, and their principal farinaceous food to-day consists in the yam (*Dioscorea*), which becomes from four to eight feet in length, and in the dalo, a caladium, which grows in swampy places. In time of harvest they often bury the breadfruit, dalo or bananas in pits lined thickly with leaves and covered with earth and with stones to foil the pigs. Treated thus, the fruit ferments and may remain for months before being cooked and eaten. Famine is indeed all but impossible in the high islands of the tropical Pacific.

In the rich soil of the broad Rewa valley sugarcane is cultivated extensively. Cotton becomes a perennial tree in Fiji and produces an exceptionally good quality of boll. Delicious pineapples grow on the less fertile soils, and coffee thrives on the mountain slopes. Indeed, had the Fijis but a market for their produce, they would outstrip Hawaii as centers of agricultural industry.

Even in savage days the natives delighted to cultivate flowers, and the chiefs wore garlands of blossoms around their heads as do the young men and maidens of to-day. It was by means of the flowers that they knew the months, for the scarlet blooms of *Erythrina* marked the season for the planting of crops. June was heralded by the "tombebe" flowers along the shore, and when the ivi with its violet-scented flowers bloomed in the forest, the natives watched, knowing that it was nearing November when upon the morning of the moon's last quarter the water over the reef would be crowded by myriads of the Mbalolo worms swimming only to burst and shrivel with the rising of the sun, thus casting forth their eggs into the sea, after which the worms, emptied of eggs, sink as mere translucent skins to die upon the bottom. This was the great feast of the Mbalolo, the New Year's Day of former times, when bearers would be despatched to carry the cooked worms nicely wrapped in leaves to far-off chiefs among the mountain valleys.

*A MAIDEN OF KAMBARA. FIJI. Type of the Viti-Tonga race.*

Once from an old man I gathered a myth of the Mbalolo to the effect that long ago their ancestors were sailing over the sea, while one of the sea-gods guarded the canoe and each day sent food in the form of the Mbalolo, but one old man, fearing it might not be continued, collected more than was required for the day and hid it beneath a mat. Whereupon the god visited the canoe and detected the Mbalolo through the odor arising from its decomposition. In a rage, he swore never again to provide food for the ingrates; but the old man taunted him, saying that the real reason was he had lost the power to cause the worms to appear. Thus, in order to show that he still had power to produce it, the Mbalolo is permitted to swarm only upon the mornings of the last day of the October, and especially of the November moon. Accordingly, October is called *Vula i Mbalolo leilei* (the moon of the little Mbalolo) and November *Vula I Mbalolo levu* (the moon of the Great Mbalolo). In Samoa, this worm is called Palolo from *Pa,* to burst, and *lolo,* oily, referring to the oily appearance of the water when myriads of the worms burst and cast forth their eggs.

I suspect this myth to be of recent origin, for it bears a suspiciously close resemblance to the manna story in the Bible. Moreover, the old Fijian mythology asserts that their original ancestors were created in Fiji and did not sail over the ocean to these islands. It is remarkable how quickly a new myth may arise among a simple people. Certain floods which occurred within the century have passed into mythology, and one of the mountain tribes has a song of the marvellous manner in which sugar is made at the recently established sugar mill on the Rewa river. A tower of Babel myth has arisen since the conversion to Christianity, and, in Tahiti, a recently originated folk story tells of the creation of the first woman *Ivi* from a bone of the first man.

The Fijians are of mixed stock. Their dark brown skin, thick mop-like heads of hair, broad noses, and full lips betoken Papuan ancestry of remote African origin, and probably the earliest inhabitants were of purer Negroid blood than those of the present, for there has been a constant admixture with the Polynesians, who, being good navigators, have peopled the remote islands of the outer Pacific. For ages this admixure has been checked through the practice of the Fijians of killing and eating strangers who were stranded upon their shores, and it is interesting to see that it is only in the small islands of the Lau group of the Fiji archipelago that a decided mingling of the Papuan and Polynesian elements is observed. These Lau islands are set one after another, like the leeward isles of the West Indies, in a long sweeping crescent along the eastern edge of the archipelago, and are only about 270 miles west of Tonga, hence the Tongans, under their great chief Maafu, overran them, killing the men and capturing the women, and producing a tall, fine-featured, brown-skinned "Vititonga" race, far superior to the negroid peoples of the western islands of the Fijis.

*WOMEN OF FIJI. The long uncut locks indicate that a woman is unmarried.*

*Natives of Kambara Island, Fiji.*

In Fiji, as elsewhere in the Pacific, the strongest natives live along the shore where coral reefs and cocoanuts afford abundant and varied food. At times these shore tribes welcomed the coming of Tongans among them, for they are far better navigators and more intelligent than the Papuans of ancient Fiji, and they taught the art of canoe building. Indeed, pigs and chickens and certain vegetables are thought to have been introduced by this back wave of Polynesian immigration from Tonga.

Among the mountain valleys of Viti Levu one may still see traces of the stunted, sooty-skinned, long-armed, mop-headed negroid race of old Fiji, while in the eastern parts of the group and along the fertile coasts the natives are superior both mentally and physically. The average height of the chiefs is fully six feet, they stand superbly erect, no student's stoop disfiguring the proud shoulders of these noblemen of nature's making. The skin is rich bronze-brown, the lips full, but not protrusive, the nose not especially flattened, and the hair alone remains African and grows into a huge stiff mop which they periodically cover with lime, causing it to lose its black color and to assume a tawny brown-red hue. The eye lacks the languid softness of the Polynesian's and is small, swine-like and often bloodshot, imparting a cruel aspect to the visage.

Yet, withal, the native grace and unconscious dignity of these superb people, especially those of chieftain's rank, produces a profound impression. Physically they seem to be a finer race than we, yet they lack the endurance of the Caucasian, and soon succumb to prolonged assumed the character of a veritable plague, more than one quarter of the population perishing, while in many villages the children starved, and the dead were devoured by hogs, for none were left to bury them.

Yet we must come to the tropical Pacific to see how beautiful the human form may be. As Wilkes wrote, "I have scarcely seen, a finer looking set of men than composed the suite of Tanoa" (King of Fiji); and Miss Gordon Cumming spoke truly when she said that no English duchess bore herself with greater dignity and graciousness of mien than did the ladies of the royal family of Mbau.

In many another trait do they show their kinship to the universal feminine. Wilkes attempted to entertain the Queen of Rewa and her maids of honor on the *Vincennes,* but nothing seemed to please, and the party was evidently drifting into failure until, upon a whispered word from the Queen, all became animated and lively expressions of delight changed the entire tone of the afternoon. It transpired later that the Queen had commanded her suite to "act as if pleased."

*MBAU, FIJI, from a hill above the town, 1899.*

Their scantiness of attire serves but to reveal the beauty of their forms. Indeed, we must recall the fact that even in cannibal days the Fijians would never expose the entire body, for such immodesty would have merited death at the hands of the chief, and in 1837 the natives of Levuka sent off a deputation to protest to Captain Dumont d'Urville against the indecency of his sailors in entering the ocean stripped of clothing. Dress has little or nothing 'to do with morality; indeed, among savage people the more clothing they are forced to assume the lower do their morals decline. Dressed in his simple waist-cloth, the Fijian is ready at any moment to seek the deep pools of some cool mountain stream in which to bathe. As civilization introduces clothing, so does this practice of swimming decline, and the once cleanly native becomes the prey of filth-diseases. Fortunately, the British Governments of Papua and Fiji have not insisted upon the hat, shirt and trousers for the men, or the ugly "mother hubbards" for the women, which the missionaries have forced upon the natives of nearly all other groups in the Pacific, to the detriment of both health and morals.

As James Chalmers, the great missionary to Papua, wrote in 1885

Syphilis and strong drink have received the blame for the deterioration and extinction of native races, but I think the introduction of clothing has done much in this direction. To swathe their limbs in European clothing spoils them, deteriorates them, and I fear hurries them to premature death. Put excessive clothing with syphilis and strong drink and I think we shall be nearer the truth. Retain native customs as much as possible—only those which are very objectionable should be forbidden—and leave it to the influence of education to raise them to purer and more civilized customs.

The Polynesians of Samoa, Hawaii, Tahiti and New Zealand had a lyric history sung by priests and sagas which told of days when the ancestors of their chiefs were gods, but the Melanesian race has little of this mythology, and there is no "history" in Fiji, where, according to Wilkes, all are said to have descended from a single pair, whom the gods made black and wicked and to whom they gave but little clothing. Then the gods made the brown-skinned Tongans who behaved better and to whom they gave more clothing, and, last of all, the white men were created, and these were well behaved and were given much clothing. There are apparently no myths of ancient migrations, and the people are said always to have lived in Fiji.

There is no history of the group as a whole, for war was the one chief object of Fiji, and each little district was forever suspicious of its neighbors. Indeed, to such a degree did the Fijians carry their zest for war that two men would walk abreast, never one behind the other, for the temptation of the man behind to club his companion might at any moment become irresistible. It was death to pass behind a chief or to cross his shadow, or the shadow of his house. No Fijian revenge was assuaged until the enemy was eaten; indeed, so natural does this seem to them that a high chief asked me in a casual manner whether we of the

United States had eaten the Spaniards whom we had killed during the war of 1898.

A detailed account of the ceaseless native wars is given by the Reverend Joseph Waterhouse in "The King and People of Fiji" and by Williams in his fascinating "Fiji and the Fijians" and they are records of treachery, murder, cruelty and vice, unrelieved by the narration of a single fight for principle or an act of mercy or chivalry. In all history there have been few instances of higher courage, fidelity and devotion to their creed than those furnished by the lives of the early missionaries to these islands, and nowhere in the Pacific has conversion accomplished more good and in the process done less harm than in Fiji.

Tradition states that in former times the island of Mbengha was dominant in native affairs, and its chiefs still style themselves "Qalicuva-ki-lagi," "subject only to heaven"; finally, however, the chief of Rewa conquered Mbengha and slaughtered nearly all its inhabitants, and then, in 1800, the village of Verata on Viti Levu became dominant in Fijian affairs. At this time, Mbanuvi, who had succeeded his father Nailatikau, was the head chief of the town of Mbau, but he soon thereafter died and was succeeded by his son, Na Ulivou (The Hot Stone).

Mbau is a little island, not a mile in width, which lies off the southeastern corner of the great island of Viti Levu, of which indeed it is a mere outlyer, being connected with the mainland at low tide by a natural causeway. Yet this insignificant islet of a single hill, surrounded by shallow mangrove flats and reefs, was destined to conquer nearly half of Fiji.

In the south seas that chief who first obtained the aid of white men in the use of firearms gained a rapid and terrible ascendency. It so happened that in 1809 the armed brig *Eliza* was wrecked on the coral reef off Nairai, which was a dependency of Mbau, and the natives plundered the vessel. A Swede, named Charley Savage, and three companions made their way to the shore, and Savage was the. first white man to come to Mbau. Here it is not improbable that he would have been killed and eaten in accordance with Fijian custom respecting the shipwrecked, had he not bethought himself of a musket which had been left on board, and requested the natives to search for it. They found it, built into the palisade surrounding a native village and soon Na Ulivou saw in Savage and his musket the means to "world-wide" conquests.

Verala, which was only eight miles from Mbau, was then the strongest power in Fiji, dominating the villages for about ten miles along the shore of Viti Levu, but Mbau, aided by this base imitator of Champlain, soon stripped it of its dependencies, leaving to its chief only his native village. Savage caused the natives to construct an arrow proof sedan chair, within which he remained comfortably seated firing through an opening, and this contrivance was carried into battle while he terrified and slaughtered the impotent enemies of Mbau. For his share of the spoils of conquest Savage demanded women, and he is said to have acquired a hundred wives. Na-Ulivon heaped honors and titles upon him and gave him for his principal wife a chieftainess of the highest rank, but her children were strangled for reasons of state polity, so that after his death he was survived by but a single daughter.

For two years Mbau enjoyed a monopoly of firearms in Fiji, and conquered all the neighboring islands and overran the eastern and southern coasts of Viti Levu, Finally, in 1813, the Mbauan conquests were pushed as far as Mbua in the southwestern part of Viti Levu, where in a fierce battle the ammunition of Savage and his white companions became exhausted, and they were forced to retreat to a small island in the river, where they were surrounded by thousands of howling enemies engaged in devouring the bodies of the fallen warriors of Mbau. Savage went to the water's edge to treat for terms of surrender, where he was captured, drowned and eaten, and his leg bones made into sail needles, while other parts of his skeleton were ground into powder to be drunk in Yaqona.

*RATU BEM TANOA AND HIS WIFE AUI CAKABAU IN THEIR HOUSE AT NAVUSO. VITI LEVU ISLAND, FIJI, IN 1899. They are cousins, both being members of the Royal Family of Fiji. The screen is a large piece of Taviuni tapa.*

In 1814, Na-Ulivou and his warriors again came to Mbua with a great fleet of war-canoes, and wreaked terrible vengeance upon those who had killed their champion Savage. For long years after this no native would pass the spot where Savage died without first plucking some leaves and casting them upon the ground; for, as Williams says

the Fijian peoples with invisible beings every remarkable spot: the lonely dell, the gloomy cave, the desolate rock, and the deep forest. Many of these he believes are on the alert to do him harm; therefore in passing their territory he throws down a few green leaves to propitiate the demon of the place.

In the South Seas the most dreaded ghost is that of the man who seeks revenge for having been murdered and devoured.

Early in his reign a powerful conspiracy arose against Na-Ulivou, but he drove the rebel chiefs from Mbau and also from Rewa, whither they had retreated, and finally he pursued them to Somo Somo on Taviuni, whence they fled to the distant island of Lakemba, whither he met them in a great sea fight and they were utterly annihilated. After this, Na-Ulivou assumed the title of Vunivalu (root of war), and he reigned the greatest chief in Fiji until his death in 1829.

Rewa, however, remained independent of Mbau, and indeed until the group was annexed to Great Britain these two villages were rivals almost constantly at war.

In about 1804 a number of convicts who had escaped from Australia settled upon Rewa and were protected by its chief, and the aid rendered by these reprobates was sufficient to prevent Mbau from conquering Rewa. Even in Fiji, where cruelty, treachery, cannibalism and ferocity were considered virtues, some of these men are still remembered as monsters of iniquity. In a few years they had nearly all killed one another or fallen in native wars, and only one, Paddy Connel, called Berry by the Fijians, survived until 1841, and served as guide, pilot and interpreter to Wilkes during the surveying operations of the United States Exploring Expedition in 1840. This man became thoroughly Fijianized, having the traditional hundred wives and forty-eight children, and so great was his influence that the chief of Rewa would always roast and eat any man who incurred Connel's displeasure. Indeed, if native accounts are to be trusted, Connel was himself a cannibal. All travelers in the Pacific will agree that the most vicious savage is not the native, but the degenerate white who has violated his birthright to civilization.

When na-Ulivou of Mbau died, he was succeeded by his brother Tanoa (kava bowl), who reigned for twenty-three troubled years, and died a cannibal and a heathen in 1852.

Soon after Tanoa's accession, a powerful faction in Mbau decided to make war upon Rewa. This Tanoa was desirous of preventing, for he was Vasu (nephew) to Rewa, his mother having been a chieftainess of this place. This gave him the right to seize and appropriate to his own use almost anything he desired from Rewa, where he was treated with a respect bordering upon religious adoration; for whenever he visited his mother's district the people would salute him with clapping of hands and shouting "Hail good is the coming hither of our noble lord nephew."

Naturally he was well disposed toward Rewa and he treacherously aided them while ostensibly prosecuting the war. This enraged the Mbau chiefs and they drove him into exile, where he remained five years, but finally in 1837 with the aid of his son Seru (afterwards called Thakombau) he reconquered his native village, and in a fiendish orgy dismembered his captives, roasting and eating their tongues, arms and legs while they still lived.

Beneath every post of his house in Mbau a slave was buried when his new canoes were launched they were rolled into the water over the bodies of living victims who, after being crushed, were roasted and eaten, and when the canoe took to the water men were slain upon its deck so that it might be baptized in blood. When he sailed, he ran down all in his path, often capturing the victims for his cannibal feasts, for it was the rule in Fiji that all who were upset or wrecked were regarded as sacrifices to the gods. Indeed, the gods of Fiji were themselves cannibal ghosts of dead chiefs and fed upon the spirits of those who were sacrificed.

Wilkes gives a description of the coming of Tanoa to a conference held upon the U. S. S. *Vincennes* in August, 1840;

The canoe of Tanoa, the king of Mbau, was discovered rounding the southern point of the island of Ovalau; it presented a magnificent appearance with its immense sail of white mats; the pennants streaming from its yard denoting it as belonging to some great chief. It was a fit accompaniment to the magnificent scenery around, and advanced rapidly and gracefully along; it was a single canoe, one hundred feet in length, with an outrigger of large size ornamented with two thousand five hundred of the Cypræa ovula shells; its velocity was almost inconceivable, and everyone was struck with the adroitness with which it was managed and landed upon the beach.

Often when Tanoa returned to Mbau from his murderous raids children yet alive were to be seen suspended by an ankle or wrist from the yardarm of this canoe, and so common was this practise that such were called in derision Mianu-manu-ni-latha (birds of the sail).

The later years of this inhuman monster were disturbed by dissentions and by the rebellions of his sons. Yet when he came to die he smiled with his last breath when told that five of his wives were to be strangled to accompany him into the world beyond.

Throughout his reign, Rewa and Mbau were almost constantly at war, but every now and then Tanoa would command the Rewa chiefs to come to Mbau to beg pardon for their temerity, which they always did, even if victorious.

Tanoa lived to be nearly if not quite eighty years of age, a rare occurrence in Fiji, for they believed that as they were at the time of death so would they be in the world to come. Thus doubly did they dread the infirmities of age, and people who passed middle life commonly requested their nearest relative and friends to strangle or bury them alive. Thus died the great chief Tuithakau (king of the reefs) of Somo somo, an event of which the missionary Williams gives a detailed and graphic description. Tuithakau was described by Commodore Wilkes as

a fine specimen of a Fiji Islander; bearing no slight resemblance to our ideas of an old Roman. His figure was particularly tall and manly and he had a head fit for a monarch. He looks as if he were totally distinct from the scenes of horror that are daily taking place around him, and his whole countenance has the air and expression of benevolence.

In August, 1845, this old aristocrat became feeble after prolonged illness, and one day he announced to those around him that the time of his death had come. Two of his wives were then adorned in gala attire and strangled by their kindred, while the old king was covered with charcoal pigment, the chieftain's turban of masi placed upon his head, and a string of whale's teeth around his neck. Then the chief priest blew two blasts upon his triton shell, and after an interval turning to the old king's son he said "True the sun of one king has set, but our king yet lives." Then the aged man was carried out through an opening torn through the wall of the house, as is the custom to-day at Fijian funerals, and they placed him upon the bodies of his two dead wives who lay upon the mats within the grave, and as the earth was thrown over him he was heard to cough beneath the ground. Sixty of his subjects then cut off their little fingers, fastened them upon reeds and thrust them into the thatch along the eaves of the dead chief's house. So respected was this custom of burying the aged that for a whole year at Somo Somo the missionaries heard of but one natural death of an adult, and Wilkes says that among over 200 natives at Savu Savu he saw not one over forty years of age.

## Part II

Upon the death of old Tanoa, his son Thakombau (evil to Mbau) became Vunivalu. He was an ambitions, energetic, crafty and intelligent man, but the problems of government were becoming yearly more complex in Fiji.

Missionaries had entered the group in 1835, and although Tanoa did not permit them to live in Mbau or to attempt to make converts of his subjects, other chiefs welcomed them, for they brought valuable presents and increased the importance of those among whom they lived. Gradually other white men had come to Fiji. At first mere degenerates or deserters from vessels who lived as did the natives themselves, but afterwards men of more ambition and intelligence gathered to the shores of these distant islands, and assumed a leading part in affairs. The missionary influence was beginning to be felt, for converts were being made among the lower orders of the population, and the power of the native priests, and with it that of the chiefs was weakening.

Vainly did Thakombau rail against the advance of civilization, for the hated power of the Mbau chief, founded as it was upon terrorism, was doomed. One after another defeats came to the war parties of Thakombau, and so reduced was he at last that, the missionaries being the sole power left to whom he could appeal for aid, he was forced in 1854 to profess Christianity, and cannibal feasts were known no more at Mbau. It was a great triumph for the missionaries, the result of nineteen years of unremitting toil amid constant dangers and surroundings unspeakable in horror.

That Thakombau's conversion was forced upon him as a matter of expediency is evident, for in a speech he called upon the gods of Fiji, saying that he still respected them as of old, but that the time had come when he must add the white man's god to those of his ancestors.

In the days of his power he had owned a fleet of more than a hundred war canoes, manned by a thousand warriors. 15,000 subjects acknowledged him as king, and in addition half of Fiji paid him tribute or admitted his supremacy, and he had boasted that the cannibal ovens of Mbau never grew cold. He had more than fifty wives, and he himself knew not how many children, and when but a child he had wantonly murdered one of his playmates;

yet he had but to declare himself a Christian and hundreds of his subjects followed the chief's example as Fijian custom demanded. Indeed, even to-day whenever a high chief stumbles and falls all in his neighborhood must tumble like checkers in a row, and, if he takes medicine, his subjects clamor for some of the same sort.

We must not assume that all or even that most of the Fijians were hypocrites in thus following their chief. For years the zealous spirit of the missionaries had been at work among them and they had gained the hearts of many of the poor and downtrodden, especially of the women, upon whom the tyranny of savage days fell with a heavy hand. It was the high chief and the warrior classes who had most to lose through the levelling democracy of Christianity which denied their divine right to rule through tabu, abolished their polygamy, discouraged war, prohibited cannibalism and in every way lessened their authority and rendered ridiculous the proud traditions of their caste. While the high chief remained unconverted, the missionary's lot was happy in that he well could be the kind and simple friend of the distressed and the brotherly adviser of the troubled, but with the conversion his temporal power became paramount, for it was impossible for him to escape the difficult double role of leader in secular as well as religious affairs, and thus the simple-minded lover of mankind was suddenly exalted into the position of the vicar of the terrible god of the white man whose favor was hard to win and whose punishments were eternal.

It is but fair to the missionaries to recognize that their temporal tower was at the outset forced upon them, and that the mistakes which they have at times fallen into are those which overshadow the spiritual function of the clergy in all states wherein the government has fallen under the domination of the priesthood.

It was indeed fortunate for Fiji that the missionaries had been obliged to labor for nineteen long and almost hopeless years, and to endeavor in every way to understand and endear themselves to the people before any of the important chiefs had yielded to their teaching.

Everywhere in the Pacific where missionary success was quickly and easily attained, results more or less disastrous to the natives had followed. Despite many notable and glorious exceptions such as Chalmers of Papua, the old type of missionary was too often predisposed to regard all customs not his own as "heathen," hence pernicious. Thus if his success was immediate, as in Hawaii, his well-meant zeal impelled him too quickly to overthrow old customs and at once to force upon his converts a semblance of the habits of his own stratum of European society.

In this connection it should, however, be said that the blame for most of the bigotry, which has been all too evident, especially in former times, should fall but lightly if at all upon the field worker who, living among the natives, comes to love them as his friends and at least deals with them as individuals; but the fault lies chiefly with the home boards, who, not realizing the paramount importance of local conditions in treating with primitive peoples, have attempted to enforce almost the same set of regulations from Greenland's icy mountains to Africa's coral strand.

The missionary, whether he would or no, is forbidden to conduct marriages between heathen and Christians, and too often one party to the contract must enter upon it with a lie upon his or her lips. The hypocrisy and espionage which results from sharing with the informer, or the chief, the fines derived from those who smoke, or swear, or work upon a Sunday, may well be imagined, and moreover, altogether too large a share of the earned wealth of the natives is demanded from them, the revenues of the church in certain groups being decidedly larger than the taxes collected by the civil government.

Yet let us not blind ourselves to an appreciation of the fundamental good the missions have accomplished, for whether Christianity be true or false, the natives must live under the rule of a people actuated by its motives and its faith, and are thus through its acquisition inestimably better fitted to resist the evil that preys upon them with the advent of "civilization."

In Fiji, however, the natives had become thoroughly known to the missionaries before the great conversion of 1854, and many old customs were thus permitted to remain which would have been suppressed had the missionary, and the political party which inevitably springs up around him, came more quickly into power.

The *power* of the missionary, after the great chiefs cast in their lot with him, is indeed terrible for good or evil, and in Tonga and later in Fiji he connived at the arming of the natives in order to *conquer* "converts." As the struggling priest of a great religion the missionary inspires all respect, but as the crafty politician or bigoted inquisitor his actions become correspondingly reprehensible. Too often in those early days of missionary endeavor he seemed satisfied with a mere semblance of order and religion for this was the period in which faith rather than good works was deemed essential. To the natives he too often remained one of a foreign race—a wizard, terrible, mysterious and implacable. Happily, a change has come over the thought of the world, and the conditions we describe are not those of to-day.

Henceforth Thakombau was to remain nominally king in Fiji, but the real power was vested in the white men who had settled upon his shores. He had escaped the retribution of native revenge only to struggle hopelessly in the net of commercialism and diplomacy. It was a sad and disappointing period between the time of the conversion in 1854 and the annexation to Great Britain in 1874. Soon after Thakombau "lotued"-in 1854, a powerful faction in Mbau rebelled and fled to Rewa where they arrayed themselves under the banner of the great chief Ratu Quara or Tui Dreketi (the Hungry Woman or the Long Fellow), a famous warrior and an implacable enemy of Thakombau who threatened to destroy Mbau and to kill and eat its king in revenge for the burning of Rewa in 1847. At one time only a single Tongan and a missionary guarded Thakombau in his house at Mbau, but, at this critical juncture, an American ship under Captain Dunn arrived and, aided by the missionaries, Thakombau and his party were enabled to purchase guns and ammunition. Rewa might still have conquered, however, had it not been that Ratu Quara died of dysentery in January, 1855.

Indeed, as the Reverend Mr. Waterhouse states, the people of Mbau grew to hate Christianity after Thakombau had professed it to be his religion. The Fijians had a highly developed system of constitutional government, which varied somewhat with the locality, but was nowhere an absolute despotism. In fact the influence of unprincipled white men and the introduction of firearms led to conquests which had done more to exalt the power of a few chiefs and to develop the worst excrescences of the social and religious system of Fiji than had any other factor.

At Mbau there were two high chiefs, the head priest of Roko Tui (the reverenced king) who was above all in rank and was held in religious veneration but took no part in war or political affairs; and the Vunivalu (root of war), the executive head of the tribe. Upon the death of the Vunivalu, his successor was elected from among his relatives by the land-owners and chiefs of the tribe, and should he fail to carry out their policy they refused to provide him with food.

After white men came and the lust for conquest overpowered all else at Mbau, their ancestral veneration for the Roko Tui declined, and the Vunivalu became correspondingly more powerful. Thus Thakombau was not the Mikado but the Tycoon of his people.

But to return to the historic narrative: King George Tubou of Tonga, the most powerful Christian convert in the Pacific, came to the aid of Thakombau in 1855, and for the moment reestablished his supremacy, but at the same time he acquired a knowledge of Thakombau's weakness, and became convinced that a Tongan conquest of Fiji was possible.

For generations the Tongans had been in the habit of sailing to Lakemba, Kambara, and other islands of the Lau group in Fiji, where the forests afforded large trees for the making of canoes. A year or more would be employed in canoe building, and thus the newcomers had learned Fijian customs and acquired an interest in the political affairs of the islands. Finally they began to overrun and conquer the Fijians and were the cause of much disorder and distress.

In about 1848 a powerful rebellion headed by Maafu the cousin of the Christian king broke out in Tonga, but was suppressed by George Tubou.

Maafu, its leader, was exiled to Fiji and it was intimated to him that if he desired a kingdom it was his to conquer.

Of the highest Tongan birth, young, ambitious, of superb physique, energetic and in every sense a leader among men of action, Maafu came to Fiji and at once became the ruler of all Tongans in the group.

His policy was to assist the weaker Fijian chiefs at war with stronger enemies, and then the combined Tongan and Fijian army having been victorious, he would turn upon his erstwhile allies and overpower them. Thus he gained a foothold at Vanua Mbalavu and from this as a base he proceeded to conquer the Fijis. As Seeman says in his account of his Government Mission to Fiji:

Where Maafu and his hords had been it was as if a host of locusts had descended.

Famine and poverty stalked in his wake, yet wherever he went there was a Tongan "teacher" by his side; and, as Seeman says,

the Wesleyan missionaries were kept quiet by Maafu making it the first condition in arranging articles of peace that the conquered should renounce heathenism and become Christians.

There is a strange silence in missionary accounts respecting Maafu, for not once does his name appear in Calvert's "Missionary Labors among the Cannibals" published in 1870, yet he added hundreds of "converts" to their flocks, and the Tongans and missionaries remained upon the best of terms; and only after the treacherous and brutal torture and massacre of prisoners at Natakala and Naduri were the missionaries forced by outraged public opinion to wash their hands of Maafu and join weakly in the protest against Tongan cruelty. It seems almost incomprehensible that this sad and revolting abuse of power should have been exhibited by the missionaries in the part they took in conniving at native warfare in Tonga Tahiti, and Fiji in order that their reports to the home mission might "glow with the glorious story of conversions."

By 1858 there were but two great chiefs left in Fiji, Maafu and Thakombau, and the two powers were face to face. Doubtless the missionaries would have had their own way more readily with Maafu, for when they had suggested to Thakombau the abolition of the old system and the establishment of a "constitutional monarchy," he had answered "I was born a chief and a chief I will die." Nevertheless he was finally forced into yielding to the demands of the white men. Thus Maafu "the Christian" would doubtless have conquered Mbau and become king of all Fiji had not Thakombau in 1858 signed a deed of cession granting his possessions to Great Britain. The British consul, William Pritchard, Esq., and a warship came to his aid, and Maafu was checked; and although the negotiations with England came to nought, the increasing immigration of Europeans to Fiji made native warfare more and more infrequent. Maafu had to content himself with only a partial realization of his ambition and in 1882 he died a disappointed man. Had he commenced his operations five years sooner, he would have become the conquerer of Fiji. It was the hand of Great Britain, not that of the missionaries, that had checked his blood stained career.

The affair which caused Thakombau most serious trouble appears to have been one of those extortions which have been so frequently perpetrated by a "civilized" upon a simple people. On July 4, 1849, the residence of a whiter trader named Williams, then serving as United States consul in Fiji, was burned and the natives stole some of the furniture and stores while the house was in flames. Thakombau does not appear to have been personally responsible for the firing of the house, but the natives of Mbau in which the incident occurred were subject to him, and

Williams demanded from Thakombau about $3,000 as indemnity. Upon the king's refusing to pay, the consul's demands were gradually increased and other claimants appeared, so that finally, having secured the cooperation of the United States government, the sum of $45,000 was demanded. Utterly unable to meet this "indemnity," harassed at home, and threatened from abroad, it seemed to simple Thakombau an intervention of Providenece when certain money-lenders from Australia offered to pay the claim of the United States in consideration of the deeding to them of 200,000 acres of the best land in Fiji. It may well be imagined that only for a brief moment was his kingly head allowed to rest in peace. Poor Thakombau, and with him all Fiji, had indeed fallen "into the hands of the Jews," and it was a happy moment when, on October 10, 1874, he signed a document which read, "We, King of Fiji, together with other high chiefs of Fiji, hereby give our country, Fiji, unreservedy to her Britannic Majesty, Queen of Great Britain and Ireland. And we trust and repose fully in her that she will rule Fiji justly and affectionately, that we may continue to live in peace and prosperity." Never was the confidence of a poor and degraded people better requited by a rich and civilized one, for a strong, and generous hand had come to rule in Fiji and the light of a happier day dawned upon the oppressed. Sir Arthur Gordon (afterwards Lord Stanmore) was the first British governor. He had witnessed the cruelties of the disastrous native war in New Zealand, and knew full well how difficult it is to graft a European civilization upon a Polynesian stock. Fortunately there were high-principled men to whom he could turn for advice, and he did well in seeking the councils of Mr. John Thurston, long a resident in Fiji.

The annual poll tax of £1 per man and 4s. per woman which Thakombau's government had imposed was working ruin and death in Fiji. It was impossible for the natives to earn so large a sum, but the white planters eagerly paid the taxes and then "indentured" the wretched creatures, who were forced to work upon the plantations of their white masters at a wage so low that they toiled for 280 days in the year simply to repay the tax which the planter had paid to the government. Thus were the Fijians being entrapped into a bitter and unnatural bondage more merciless than the orgies of the worst period of cannibal days.

But Sir Arthur Gordon and Mr. Thurston soon tore loose the shackles of the slaves, despite the angry protests and threats of the whites in Fiji.

Their plan was that each district be obliged to maintain a garden of copra, cotton, candle-nuts, tobacco, coffee or other produce, or to supplement this by the manufacture of mats or other articles of trade, and at the end of each year the products were to be sold under government supervision to the highest bidder and any money received over and above that of the district tax was to be returned to the district itself and divided among the taxpayers. This simple plan, which closely accords with their ancient manner of raising tribute, has encouraged industry among the natives, shielded them from the avarice of traders, secured to them their lands, and each year produced a sum considerably in excess of the taxes.

Excellent as this plan was, it remained deficient in one important respect, for the government made no effort to establish manual-training schools wherein old crafts might be improved and new ones developed. Education in Fiji has been confined to religion and the "three K's," and inspiring as it is to witness the son of a cannibal extracting cube roots and solving quadratic equations, one inclines to the opinion that the prodigy's future life would be better assured of a career of useful service to the world and of happiness to himself had he been taught to be a good carpenter, mason, farmer or decorator. It is certainly unfortunate that, having ingeniously created a market for the products of Fijian labor, the English failed to improve the earning capacity of the natives, thus losing an unique opportunity to stimulate an interest in the useful arts that might soon have obliterated the apathy of the downcast race.

Mr. Thurston, the originator of the new system of taxation, had come to Fiji as a common sailor before the mast, but he lived to be Governor of Fiji from 1888 to 1896, and died as Sir John Thurston, universally beloved by the race for whose uplifting he had contended so courageously and well, and thus in Fiji there live to-day the happiest, the most law-abiding and potentially the most nearly civilized natives in the Pacific. It is one of the very few instances wherein a powerful and enlightened race have studied and toiled through many unrequited years to lift to a happier level a poor and barbarous people.

There is no longer in Fiji that painful contrast of which Wilkes complained between the beauty of the island scenery and the character of the inhabitants, for consistently in all respects the archipelago is now one of the fairest spots within the tropic world.

Nowhere in the Pacific did old customs change more slowly under European rule than in Fiji, for it has been the consistent policy of the British government to leave unaltered all that was good in the manners of old days.

The villages are almost as they were before the white man came, only the log stockades and the encircling moats have disappeared during the long years of peace, and the houses are no longer perched upon the summits of ærie cliffs, but now cluster along the river-banks or under the cocoa palms of the seashore. The high-peaked Mbures or temples, once such a picturesque feature, have fallen into decay with the advent of Christianity, although one thinks they might well have been preserved, enlarged and converted into Christian churches, for the tasteful sennit patterns which adorned their beams and rafters would have made the chapel the most attractive house in the village instead of being, as it too often is, a cheerless barn-like structure, ill-proportioned without and barren within.

The better types of native houses are set upon artificial embankments of stones and earth, sometimes twenty feet high, as in the valley of the Rewa River, where floods may be expected. The framework is of tree fern or cocoanut logs, ingeniously lashed together, and the sides and roof are covered with a thick thatch of wild cane, or cocoanut leaves spread over ferns. The roof is quite thin at the peak, but is fully a foot and a half thick at the eaves, where it projects slightly, and is cut off squarely, presenting a very neat appearance. The ground-plan of the house is usually rectangular, not oval at its ends, as in Tahiti, and the peaked roof has a long ridge-pole which projects several feet beyond the eaves and, if the residence be that of a chief, is thickly studded with white *Cyprœa* cowrie shells, and sometimes other cowrie shells are strung upon ropes of cocoanut fiber sennit and hung pendant from the projecting ridge-pole. There are no windows, but several openings serve as doors and may in time of rain be closed with mats. The floor is covered with several layers of pendamu mats, and a raised dais at one end of the single room serves as a bed and may be screened by mosquito-proof curtains of masi (tapa). A rectangular earth-covered depression serves for the fireplace and the smoke escapes as best it may, the smoldering embers imparting always a pleasant aroma to the air.

In speaking of everything Fijian, we must remember that the peoples of the Ra, or western islands of the Archipelago, and of the mountains, are of purer Papuan stock and are more primitive than those of the Vititonga race of the Lau group and the eastern coasts of the large island. Accordingly, the houses differ in different places, being smaller, more crudely and flimsily made among the Papuan than among the Vititonga tribes. Also in the western parts of the large islands and in the Ra islands, the chiefs are not so highly respected as among tribes whose blood has been mingled with the aristocratic Polynesian. At Mbau, the Roko Tui was almost god-like in native estimation, whereas in the mountains of Vita Levu the chief was only the leading councilor of the tribe, and labored in the fields in common with his subjects. Indeed the Mbau chiefs looked down upon those of the western part of Viti Levu, calling them Kai-si (peasants).

If the house were that of a high chief, as at Mbau or Rewa, the roof-beams were wrapped with interlacing strands of cocoanut fiber sennit, displaying a pattern in rich browns, black and yellow, so pleasingly contrasted that one is forced to regret that work of such high artistic merit should be suffered to remain in a house as inflammable as a haystack. Yet these houses withstand a hurricane far better than do the hideous corrugated-iron-roofed structures of Europeans.

Several old wooden basins, yaqona bowls, are hung upon the wall, their naturally dark wood coated with pearly blue where many a brewing of the drink has stained them. Carved war-clubs and long elaborately decorated spears may be seen suspended from the beams, and as the eye becomes accustomed to the dim light one beholds such treasures as a sperm whale's tooth strung as were old-fashioned powder horns upon a rope of cocoanut fiber and polished through repeated rubbings with cocoanut oil until its surface is as brown as tinted meerschaum. A few fly-brushes, pandamus fans for awakening the fire, a huge ceremonial war-fan of palm-leaf, some wooden food bowls, and crude cooking pots of fire-baked clay, and a clock that never goes, complete the list of the furniture. Yet one thing of painful memory one would fain have overlooked—the universal pillow. This consists of a block of wood or stick of bamboo supported upon legs so that it stands horizontally four or five inches above the floor. In old days when the hair was most elaborately dressed and trained into a huge mop, this pillow was doubtless a necessity, but in this shaven and shorn period of Chrisianity such an instrument of torture might well be dispensed with, although by the native it is still regarded as the acme of luxury.

Housekeeping is simple in happy Fiji, where all is charmingly clean, and thick layers of soft mats invite repose upon the floor. Indeed the natives sleep much by day, for at night there is apt to be a "meke," wherein the maidens of the village, adorned in garlands of flowers and well polished with cocoanut oil, sing far into the small hours, keeping time to their chants by graceful gestures. This, together with the dull beating of the wooden drum, drives all hope of sleep away, but it is to be preferred to the "silent" nights when rats and mice scamper ceaselessly over the floor, contesting their supremacy with an occasional centipede or land crab. Yes, one must live a life of leisure and sleep by day in Fiji.

The largest edifice in the village is called the "stranger's house" for it is here that guests are entertained and fed by the community under orders from the chief. At Mbau the old stranger's house has stood for generations, dating far back into cannibal times, and within its walls the first Christian service was held in 1854. It is about 125 feet long and 40 feet wide, being exceeded in length only by the stranger's house at Rewa.

Carpenters are a highly respected caste in Fiji, and canoe and house building are occupations fit to engage the activities of chiefs. When one desires a house, a whale's tooth or other suitable gift should be presented to the chief, who then engages the carpenters, who in turn may command the services of more than two hundred assistants, all of whom labor so efficiently that in from one to three weeks the house is erected and ready for company. In the South Seas things are done in communal fashion and village labors, such as house building, canoe making, and the gathering of crops are occasions for songs and dances and all manner of merriment and feasting.

There is much of interest in Mbau, for although the ovens have long ago grown cold, yet the great foundation stones of the old temple of the war god (Na Vatani Tawake) still remain in the center of the village, and in 1898 one could still see the sacred tree upon whose boughs were hung the genital organs of victims who had been sacrificed to the Fijian Mars.

Close by the side of the foundation of the old temple a sharp-edged column of basalt is set upright within the ground. This is the stone to which victims were dragged by their arms and upon which their heads were dashed. Fragments of human teeth might still be found by digging at the base of this stone, and in many a house in Mbau there were sail needles made from leg-bones of the victims. There was another execution stone which was axe-shaped and thrust upright into the ground near the foot of the hill; but this now serves as the baptismal font, and is set within the church. The ovens in which victims were cooked upon the hillside lay near this stone, as were also the great hollow log-drums, the "publishers of war" whose rolling beat the cannibal call in old days, and one of which now serves to summon worshippers to church.

An interesting trophy of old days was the anchor of the French brig *Aimable Josephine* which now lies close to the side of the foundation of the temple. This vessel was treacherously cut off at Mbau on the night of July 19, 1834, her captain and most of the crew being murdered. Native wars were waged over the possession of this trophy, the final resting place of which is Mbau.

The corner posts of the house of old Tanoa were still to be seen, and when natives pass these in the night they pluck green leaves and cast them upon the earth, for beneath the ground by the side of each post and embracing it with his arms there stands the skeleton of a victim who was buried alive.

The abutment of the sea wall of Mbau with its made-land, and docks built of large flat stones, is a remarkable example of native engineering, being surpassed only by the canal of the Rewans near

Nakelo. Huge canoes, some of them with bows studded with white *Cyprœa* shells, lie stranded here and there. The native houses are scattered over the made-land and along the gentle slope at the base of the hill, leaving the summit barren as of old, although here overlooking the city stands the residence of the Methodist missionary, and the graves of Tanoa and of Thakombau, the latter of whom died in 1883.

But exceeding all in interest was Ratu Epele Nailatikau, high chief of Fiji, son and successor of king Thakombau. Unreconciled to the presence of the white man, his memories harked far back to old days and beams covered with woven sennit, and in its treasures of old days, when his family were great and all-powerful in Fiji. Yet, though shorn of power, no king could have been treated with more respect by those around him than was he.

His house in Mbau was a small one, in no way differing from those of the lesser chiefs, excepting in the richness of its Taviuni tapa screens, and beams covered with woven sennit, and in its treasures of old days; the most notable of which was a well-oiled elephant's tusk beautifully browned and polished, which had lain upon the floor since the days of old Tanoa, who once prized it as the largest piece of "coin" in the world. Only the highest chiefs were permitted to enter his house, and even these dropped their titles and crouched silently against the wall awaiting his invitation ere they spoke.

In his every expression and gesture there was a stately consciousness of his high-born ancestry.

Although over sixty years of age, his finely muscular body still stood erect, with its dark bronze skin softened and smoothed through many a cocoanut-oil massage. Upon ceremonial occasions he blackened his face and covered his hair with lime. The little finger of his right hand had been severed at the first joint as an indication of mourning upon the death of his grandfather Tanoa.

RATU EPELE, HEAD CHIEF OF FIJI IN HIS HOUSE AT MBAU IN 1899. Three yagona bowls, with their strainers, are hanging upon the wall. Ratu Pope Seniloli is at his right hand, and the others are chiefs of high rank.

He was every inch a king seated in his chair with the noblest of his race crouching silently around him. Whenever he smoked a cigar he condescendingly nodded to some high chief who crawled humbly toward him on hands and knees, delighted at the honor of "finishing the butt."

When he dined, a clean new mat was unrolled upon the floor, and then men and women came crawling in on hands and knees, bearing food for the god-like one, who sat tailor-fashion upon the floor. No commoner ate in the presence of the king, and least of all would the women of his household have presumed to such familiarity. The menu of one dinner at which the author was a guest consisted in an excellent fish chowder served in cocoanut bowls, and yams placed upon four-legged wooden platters, all scrupulously clean and cooked to tempt the palate of the most fastidious epicure. Our plates were banana leaves, and fingers served in lieu of knives and forks. Cups, etc., used by the king are tabu and must not be used by others. The courtiers remained silent while the meal was in progress, only softly clapping hands when the king addressed any of their number. After dinner a bowl of water was placed before the king and the natives again clapped respectfully while he washed his hands.

Even before the advent of the white man, cooking was a high art in Fiji. In fact, these natives had little to learn from us in this direction. Their pottery enabled them to boil or steam their food, and in addition they made use of the oven. This, consists in a stone-lined pit within which a wood fire is made. Then, when the stones have become red hot the embers are raked away and the food; pigs, fish, vegetables, etc., are placed within the oven, having previously been wrapped in Tahitian chestnut or bread-fruit leaves, or in the case of man in the leaves of *Solanum anthropophagorum*, a plant allied to the potato. The food is then covered thickly with juicy green leaves which in turn are blanketed with earth. After a few hours all within the oven becomes so thoroughly baked that the ribs of pigs may be torn off and the flesh eaten as in America we do corn upon the cob.

Canoes laden with tribute (lala), for Ratu Epele were constantly arriving at Mbau. These offerings varied with the tribe, for each was charged to bring certain things. Thus one canoe might be laden with great bundles of yams, another with husked cocoanuts tied into bunches, or with yaqona root, turtles, masi, mats, etc. The greatest care was taken in the preparation of the tribute, and, in fact, the natives invariably gave the best they had.

Those who brought tribute carried it humbly to the door of the king's house and crouched close to the wall outside, softly and pleadingly clapping with their hands. Hearing the plaintive sound two chiefs of the king's household, who had hitherto been sitting motionless as statues within the room, moved to one and the other side of the door. The head of a pig, a large bunch of cocoanuts, or a turtle would then be timidly thrust part way within the opening, and a tremulous voice outside would beg that his majesty, their great and gracious lord, would condescend to accept as tribute so mean and unworthy an offering as their poverty forced them to present, trusting that in his greatness he would continue to protect and show them favor. When the voice ceased, the two chiefs at the door would critically inspect the proffered specimen of tribute, calling attention to its faults as well as to its qualities, and if its acceptance was recommended, all the chiefs who had been crouching sphinx-like against the wall within the house would show signs of life and majestically clapping their hands murmur "A! woi! woi! woi!! A tabua levu!" (a wonderfully large whale's tooth!). Upon which the king himself usually spoke a few words and the tribute was formally accepted. So abundant was this tribute that great heaps of taro, yams, cocoanuts or turtles were nearly always to be seen upon the village green of Mbau.

In the old days, wars were waged over the slightest inattention to this matter of tribute. The island of Maliki was charged to provide turtles for Tanoa, but one day they presumed themselves to eat one of the turtles they had caught; hearing of which Tanoa sent a fleet of war canoes, and every man and woman on Maliki was killed, the children being captured in order that the boys of Mbau might club them to death and thus earn their titles of Koroi (killers of men).

The old king spoke not a word of English, but he was fond of reminiscence. He remembered the *Peacock* of the Wilkes expedition, being then a boy of about 8 years. He also spoke admiringly of Professor Moseley, of the *Challenger*, and seemed saddened when told that he was dead.

The freedom with which he volunteered to discourse upon events of cannibal times was surprising. He said that one day when he was a little boy he had entered the house of Tanoa during the dinner hour, and his grandfather, who always loved him, had given him the tongue of the Mbakola (man-to-be-eaten) and its taste was vinaka (good).

After this he "often dined with his grandfather," who "had a new man nearly every day." Wilkes states that the Fijians esteemed women more highly than men, but Ratu Epele declared that the best of meat were old, lean men "whose flesh was red and whose fat was yellow," and whose taste was "like pork with bananas." Women, he declared, were "covered with a layer of fat" and white men he had been told were salty or flavored strongly with tobacco. In old days in Fiji, the highest praise one could bestow upon a dish was to liken it to a cooked man. When in Fiji, I several times overheard the remark "were it not for the English I would eat you," and in quarrelling the commonest slur is to call an antagonist (Mbakola) a man to be eaten. Our abhorrence of cannibalism, which is after all a sentimental matter in so far as the mere eating is concerned, was not shared by the old Fijians of experience, for "men are good; indeed the best of all meat," and as Ratu Epele once said "he never met a man without thinking how he would taste."

Some Fijian names for food are curious; thus bula-na-kau signifies beef, for when Captain Eagleston brought the two original cattle to Fiji he told the natives that the animals were a "bull and a cow."

Ratu Epele delighted to play at draughts with a tawny-haired albino chief whose light skin was profusely bespeckled with brown blotches and whose eyes were dull blue. This chief's function seemed to be solely that of a messenger and draught player, and invariably the games were won by the king, for no matter how great an advantage the albino might win, he "committed suicide" at the last by placing all his pieces at the mercy of his lord and master.

Ratu Epele, the most interesting chief in the Pacific, died in 1901, and with him there passed away the last champion of the old in Fiji. Born of the highest rank and to a life of war and action, fate had robbed him of his birthright and left him but dreams and memories. Like the lingering spark of a fire that can never burn again, this spirit of old cannibal days faded into oblivion. His son, the Honorable Ratu Kadavu Levu, who succeeded him as Roko Tui Tailevu, has been carefully educated under British auspices, and is a member of the Legislative council.

The cleanliness of Fijian houses is remarkable, indeed in heathen times they were far more careful in this respect than at present, for the least offal of any description, even a hair, might be used by an enemy to bewitch its originator. Even to-day the fear of witchcraft, Ndrau-ni-kau, is very real in Fiji. In order to bring ill-fortune to your enemy, you have but to discover something which he has cast off and burn it wrapped in the proper leaves, reciting certain spells. Or you may bury a cocoanut beneath his hearth, or slowly melt the wax from his image thus causing your victims lingering decline and death. The missionaries have made every effort to destroy this belief, but unfortunately they do not seek to replace it by a more wholesome understanding of the nature of filth-diseases, and thus as faith in witchcraft declines certain bodily ills increase.

In common with other south-sea islanders, the Fijians were a ceremonious people and every important affair of life was ordered in accordance with a rigid etiquette which unhappily in many instances is falling into neglect before the levelling influence of the white man's law.

Thus in the old days, the yaqona (kava of Samoa) was drunk by chiefs alone, and then only upon ceremonial occasions, but now all may partake of it and the excess thus engendered is one of the minor causes of the decline of the population. Wilkes, and also Williams, in his work on Fiji and the Fijians, describes the ceremony at Somo somo where it was most elaborate. Early in the morning the herald stood in front of the chief's house and shouted yaqona ei ava, and all within hearing responded in a shriek Mama (prepare it). Then the chiefs and priests gathered within the king's house, while all others remained at home until the king had drunk his yaqona. Pieces of the root of the *Macropiper methysticum* were distributed among the young men, who must previously have rinsed their mouths and whose teeth must be perfect. The chewed root having been deposited in the form of relatively dry pellets in the bottom of the bowl, the herald announces to the king "Sir with respect the yaqona is collected." The king replies "Loba" (wring it). The bowl is then placed before the chief, who skilfully encloses the chewed fragments of root within fibers of hibiscus or cocoanut husks and finally wrings the fluid through this sieve, thus removing from the bowl all pieces of chewed root, and leaving within it a milky-yellow brew. While the straining is progressing, the priest chants a prayer in which the company finally joins. The first cocoanut cup is always handed to the king, who pours out a few drops as a libation to the gods and then drinks while the assembled company sing, Ma-nai-di-na. La-ba-si-ye: a ta-mai ye: ai-na-ce-a-toka: Wo-ya! yi! yi! yi!, finishing with a clapping of hands and a wild shout which is passed from house to house to the uttermost limits of the village. After the king, the company is served in the order of rank until all have partaken. In old times, it is said that yaqona was grated in Fiji, but that the Tongans introduced the method of chewing. Having tried it, I must confess that the chewed root is less unpleasant in flavor than the grated, but at best it resembles a combination of quinine and camphor and is certainly an acquired taste. When drunk to excess, it temporarily paralyzes the arms and legs, at the same time exciting the brain. Thus violent quarrels are apt to occur at yaqona bouts, but the combatants are unable to injure each other. When the chief falls into a stupor the wives of the other participants carry their protesting husbands home. A dull headache upon awaking is the penalty for this over-indulgence, but the evil effects are slight in comparison with those resulting from alcoholic excesses.

The British government has, however, prevented alcoholism among the natives; for each Fijian who desires to imbibe must annually obtain a license which he is obliged to exhibit whenever he purchases a drink at any public bar, and if arrested for drunkenness his license is confiscated, not to be renewed, and moreover the bartender is heavily fined if he be detected in selling drinks to natives who possess no license.

The Fijians of to-day are more orderly and sober than, and quite as contented as are any peoples of European ancestry, and illiteracy is rarer in Fiji than in Massachusetts. You were safer even fifteen years ago in any part of Fiji, although your host knew how you tasted, than you could be in the streets of any civilized city. It is clear that in disposition the Fijians are not unlike ourselves, and only in their time-honored customs were they barbarous. Indeed the lowest human beings are not in the far-off wilds of Africa, Australia or New Guinea, but among the degenerates of our own great cities. Nor are there any characteristics of the savage, be he ever so low, which are not retained in an appreciable degree by the most cultured among us.

Yet in one important respect the savage of to-day appears to differ from civilized man. Civilized races are progressive and their systems of thought and life are changing, but the savage prefers to remain fixed in the culture of a long past age, which, conserved by the inertia of custom and sanctified by religion, holds him helpless in its inexorable grasp. Imagination rules the world, and the world to the savage is dominated by a nightmare of tradition.

It is not that there are no individuals of progressive tendencies among primitive tribes, but the careers of their Luthers and Galileos are apt to be short and to end in tragedy. Indeed, only three hundred years ago our own leaders of progress struggled at the risk of their lives against the prejudices of their contemporaries. Even with us every effort of progress engenders a counteracting force in the community which tends to check its growth and to preserve the present status, accepting the acknowledged evil of to-day to preserve the even tenor of our way, for fear of the new is akin to the superstitious dread of the unknown. Whether the race be savage or civilized depends chiefly upon the nature of the customs that are handed down as patterns upon which to mold life. and thought. The more ancient the triumph of the conservatives the more primitive the culture which is conserved, and the more likely is it to be crude and barbarous. A wonderful instance of fixity of custom is afforded by the race which in the ice-age lived in the caverns in the valleys of the Dordogne and the Vezere in central France. Their skull measurements indicate that certain of these cave-dwellers were Esquimo and their implements and works of art are the same as those of the Esquimo of the Arctic regions of to-day, who have thus remained unchanged throughout unknown thousands of years, unaffected by their great journey northward following the edge of the retreating ice.

Among all races religion is the most potent power to maintain tradition, and for the savage religion enters into every act and thought. To him as to the ancient Greeks everything is a personification of some spirit—everything is somebody. The waterfall is such, for can you not hear the laughter of the nymph, the clouds are spirits for they come and go as only gods may do, and every beast and bird and plant and stone is but the embodiment of a ghost or tribal hero.

Yet it is probable that no savage has ever been more under the dominion of a world of omens and portents than was Louis XI, and even to-day the breaking of a mirror, or the number thirteen, or a stumble while crossing a threshold, remains of significance to many of us. All matters of sentiment and credulity are closely wrapped up in this entanglement of superstition; it is hard to divorce ourselves from the idea that moving machines have life and disposition. We must perforce associate sublimity and grandeur with the inert rock-mass of the Alps, and the great trees under which we played as children are sentient beings to our imagination, and our hearts ache as for the loss of life-long friends when we find them fallen to the woodman's axe. A cold heartless world it indeed would be were we not illogical and therefore "savage" in our sentiments and loves.

Upon analysis we find that lack of sympathy for the savage and ignorance of his tradition blinds our judgment and causes us to regard as ridiculous in him things which we consider to be quite natural in ourselves. The cleverness of the Yankee who sold wooden nutmegs is quite amusing, but the Japanese who counterfeits an American trademark is criminal.

There is within us Europeans an inbred contempt for all that is alien, and this trait, being the dominant characteristic of Christian peoples, has enabled us through aggressive intolerance to impress our customs upon all other races without ourselves being influenced by the cultures we have overawed into a semblance of our own.

In strange and possibly ominous contrast with ourselves, the Japanese have for ages been keen to discover the good things of alien cultures and quick to accept them as their own, while we must remain all but unmoved by the example of their ennobling patriotism and mastery of self, the happy simplicity of their family life, their respect for worthy ancestors, their modesty, and their inbred grace of deportment; and as for their exquisite art we chiefly relegate it to our museums, and their fine chivalric code, the bushido, remains all but untranslated into our language, much less has it entered into our thought.

The savage may know nothing of our classics, and little of that which we call science, yet go with him into the deep woods and his knowledge of the uses of every plant and tree and rock around him and his acquaintance with the habits of the animals are a subject for constant wonder to his civilized companion. In other words, his knowledge differs from ours in kind rather than in breadth or depth. His children are carefully and laboriously trained in the arts of war and the chase, and above all in the complex ceremonial of the manners of the tribe, and few among us can excel in memory the priests of old Samoa, who could sing of the ancestors of Malietoa, missing never a name among the hundreds back to the far-off God Savea whence this kingly race came down.

One may display as much intelligence in tracking a kangaroo through the Australian bush as in solving a problem in algebra, and among ourselves it is often a matter of surprise to discover that men laboring in our factories are often as gifted as are the leaders of abstract thought within our universities. In fact the more we know of any class or race of men the deeper our sympathy, the less our antagonism, and the higher our respect for their endeavors. When we say we "cannot understand" the Japanese we signify that we have not taken the trouble to study their tradition.

It is a common belief that the savage is more cruel than we, and indeed we commonly think of him as enraged and of ourselves in passive mood. Child-like he surely is, and his cruelties when incensed are as inexcusable as the destruction of Louvain or the firing of Sepoys from the guns, but are they more shocking than the lynching or burning of negroes at the stake, events so common in America that even the sensational newspapers regard them as subjects of minor interest.

Clearly, despite our mighty institutions of freedom, efficient systems of public education and the devotion of thousands of our leaders to ideals of highest culture, there remain savages among us. Mere centuries of civilization combat the æons of the brute. Within each and every one of us, suppressed perhaps but always seeking to stalk forth, there lurk the dark lusts of the animal, the haunting spirit of our gorilla ancestry. The foundations of our whole temple of culture are sunken deep in the mire of barbarism. It is this fundamental fact which deceives us into the impression that a few decades of contact with men of our own race will suffice to civilize the savage. True they soon learn to simulate the manners and customs of their masters, but the imitation is a hollow counterfeit, no more indicative of enlightenment than is the good behavior of caged convicts a guaranty of high mindedness. To achieve civilization a race must conquer *itself*, each individual must master the savage within him. Cultured man has never yet civilized a primitive race. Under our domination the savage dies, or becomes a parasite or peon.

# Part III

Of all established customs in Fiji the most odious was cannibalism, yet it was always tabu for women and the lower classes, and the custom was extensively practised only by the chiefs and warriors. It is possible that in Fiji it was primitively a religious rite and did not originate in time of famine, or through motives of mere revenge. Instead of an animal, they sacrificed the best they had to the gods, and as the flesh of the animal was eaten by the chiefs, so was the flesh of man. Indeed, an old myth asserts that once there was no cannibalism in Fiji, and even when it was most prevalent there was always a party opposed to it, maintaining that it caused various skin diseases. At the town of Nakelo on the Rewa river, it was tabu to eat human flesh.

We incline, however, to the belief that the Fijians were cannibals simply because they enjoyed the taste of human flesh, for I have met with no dissent to the opinion that of all meat it is the most palatable, and it is evident that the custom could not have survived a decade had mere religion prompted its continuance. The fact appears to be that, in common with other privileges, the chiefs and priests had succeeded in monopolizing its pleasures through the agency of the tabu, for among savages the priesthood is quick to defer to the desires of those in power. In prehistoric times the natives had but little animal food, apart from the fish of the reefs and the snakes of the mountains, for pigs, ducks and chickens were introduced only recently. When man attempts to live upon a vegetable diet, even though it be varied by fish, an insatiate craving for animal food comes over him, he "Kalau's," as the natives say, and it is an interesting fact that cannibalism is almost unknown among peoples whose meat-supply has always been abundant and varied. Once it be acquired, this longing for human flesh remains a temptation haunting its possessor. Well does one remember the vim of a wild Marquesan dance. It was near midnight and the flickering glare of the bonfire cut into the blackness of the surrounding forest. An old chief, standing by the embers, led the chant, while his tribesmen, with hands joined, danced furiously around him. Translated into English, the burden of their song was "I have eaten your father, your mother, your brother, now I intend to eat you! whoo!! hack!!!"—in a bestial shriek that rang back in echoes from the cliffs. Then, one by one, at unexpected times and from unforeseen recesses, the maidens of the tribe emerged from the dark aisles among the trees; their graceful bodies glistening where the fire-light glinted upon the cocoanut oil that covered their shapely limbs. Gay flowers stood out among the riot of their flowing locks, and like elfin things they flitted with tremulous arms outstretched until they stood fully revealed in the red glare, only to flutter silently backward and vanish. In days gone by that darkness concealed from view a gruesome meal.

Basil Thomson points out the fact that in Fiji the practise increased greatly just before the coming of white men, as had that of human sacrifice among the Aztecs a few years before the arrival of Cortez. With the sudden increase in the power of the great chiefs, it began to lose its religious significance and an acknowledged appetite for cannibal meat was boastfully proclaimed. Thus Tanoa, Ra Undre-undre, Tui Kilakila, and others were cannibals because they enjoyed the taste of man, but not *all* Fijians liked human flesh, even as terrapin is not enjoyed by all white men.

The most hideous features of cannibalism were the fiendish tortures, Vaka-totogana, connected with it wherein the victims were gradually dismembered and their noses, tongues, arms, or legs cooked and eaten before their eyes, pieces of their own flesh being offered to them in derision. Even if the missionaries had accomplished nothing else, their success in abolishing cannibalism would have sanctified their labors. Let nothing blind us to an appreciation of the undaunted courage and unexcelled devotion to their faith displayed by these unselfish men and women, who, actuated by high and simple motives, left homes and friends, and labored cheerfully through long years over the seemingly hopeless task of bringing the light of a happier day to the barbarians of Fiji.

People who had died a natural death were rarely or never eaten, and only those killed in battle, captured, or wrecked "with salt water in their eyes," were offered to the gods and roasted. The dead, if killed in battle and buried, they would disinter even after the tenth day when the body could not be lifted entire from the grave and was therefore torn apart and made into puddings. Everyone agrees that decomposition did not deter their appetite for human flesh, any more than it impairs our own taste for game, yet all other meat was discarded by the Fijians as by us upon the least indication of dissolution.

Among old Fijian chiefs whom I knew between 1897-1899, none expressed the slightest abhorrence of cannibalism, and some were frank enough to state that were European influences removed they would at once renew the practise. To the Fijian no revenge is assuaged until you have eaten your enemy, but the deepest contempt for a fallen foe was indicated by roasting and then refusing to devour the body.

One of the best descriptions of a cannibal feast is that given by Jackson in Erskine's voyage published in 1853; and the Rev. Thomas William in his work upon "Fiji and the Fijians" describes the rites in detail, having often observed them.

The canoes when approaching the shore would indicate that human prey was on board by striking the water at intervals with a pole. Seeing the splashes, the natives gathered in a howling mob along the shore, the women breaking into a wild, lascivious dance. The victims were seized by the arms and dragged to the temple, their captors chanting the cannibal song:

> Yari au malua. Yari au malua.
> Drag me gently. Drag me gently.
> Oi au na saro ni nomu vanua.
> For I am the champion of thy land.

Yi mudokia! Yi mudokia! Yi mudokia!
Give thanks! Give thanks! Give thanks!
Ki Dama le!
Yi! u-woa-ai-a!

Sharp-edged strips of bamboo served as knives for the butcher, and after being roasted or steamed, the flesh was eaten by means of a wooden fork, each high chief having one of these which it was tabu for anyone but himself to touch.

Cannibalism was dreaded by the lower classes for they were forbidden to participate in the feasts, and were themselves most frequently the victims of these orgies. Thus when the missionaries succeeded in developing even in a rudimentary form the force of "public opinion" the practice was suppressed far more easily than had been anticipated, for it was a rite maintained by the aristocracy and the priests and had become a terrible engine of despotism.

Another institution which appears to have been practised from time immemorial in Fiji was polygamy. The great majority of Fijians were not polygamous, however, for only the highest chiefs could afford to maintain more than one wife, and even those of most exalted rank rarely had more than ten wives. There is reason to suppose that the number of women has always been less than that of men in Fiji, owing to the greater care devoted to the rearing of warriors.

A man of the middle classes rarely married before the age of twenty-five, at which time his mother chose a wife from among the daughters of his maternal uncle (his orthogamous cousins, veidavolani). One quarter of all Fijian marriages are still of this character, and they produce healthy offspring.

Men of the lowest class frequently remained bachelors throughout life, and all unmarried females of the peasantry were disposed of by the chief of the tribe. In Mbau this match-making chief was next in rank to the vunivalu, Thakombau. It is evident that Basil Thomson is right when he says that the abandonment of polygamy could have had no serious influence upon the vitality of the race, for it affected too few.

It is a common mistake to assume that social anarchy is the rule in primitive communities; for the reverse is true, and savage races are the ones *par excellence* most dominated by established forms, their system of life remaining unchanged for generation after generation. This is illustrated most clearly in an interesting paper by Lord Amherst of Hackney and Basil Thomson published by the Hakluyt Society of London in 1901, which shows that, since their discovery in 1568, the customs of the Solomon islanders have remained absolutely unaltered, until crushed under the rule of white men.

Among these fixed customs of savage tribes, some are actually better than our own. Thus in Fiji prostitution was checked as effectively as any mere system could prevent it. This was accomplished by obliging all the unmarried men to sleep each night in a special house, the Mbure-ni-sa, or men's house, while the virgins were kept at home with their parents.

Indeed, the use of the Mbure-ni-sa was even extended, under certain conditions, to the married men. There were no milk-producing animals in Fiji, and the food of the natives is still so deficient in animal proteids that it can hardly afford sufficient nourishment for healthy growth until the child is nearly four years old. Accordingly, when a child was born, husband and wife separated; she going to live for a year with her mother's relatives, and he to sleep for the following two or three years in the Mbure with the unmarried men. Thus throughout the suckling period the risk of a new conception was avoided, and the full strength of the mother was preserved to nourish her infant.

Unhappily, the Europeans saw fit to break up this system, maintaining that it interfered with family life and was destructive of mutual affection. The tabu having thus been abolished, conceptions often occur within a year following the birth of a child, and the mother's milk is rendered inefficient as a means of nourishment, while at the same time the drain upon her strength is so great that the unborn child may not properly develop. Thus the new system has increased the birth-rate, but at the same time produces weak, sickly infants whose death-rate is far greater than in former times. This indeed is one of the most potent causes of the decrease of the Fijian population, espcially as the married women now attempt to escape the strain of these exhausting pregnancies by resorting to abortion, a practise which has increased in recent years to the serious impairment of the vitality of the race.

Moreover, the abolition of the Mbure-ni-sa has brought about a too sudden and promiscuous commingling of the young men and women, and the commission appointed by the British government to inquire into the causes which are producing the decline of the Fijian population has decided that sexual depravity has increased since the abandonment of heathenism, for licentiousness formerly kept down by the chief's club is now merely forbidden.

Seeman states that the natives were shocked when he told them that English women frequently bore children at intervals of a year apart, and upon reflection they decided this accounted for there being so many "shrimps" (small men) among Europeans.

In common with some other primitive races, the Fijians looked frankly upon those problems of sexual relations which we attempt to ignore or to cloak under a mantle of secrecy, too often pernicious to the welfare of our race. The average European is too apt to be horrified when he hears a spade called by its simplest name, and to his mind morality implies an unnatural hypocrisy respecting the physiological facts of life. He forgets that acts and words are in themselves innocent unless their *intention* be otherwise, and in many matters of this sort the missionary has unfortunately made cowards and liars of his converts, and it is undoubtedly true that the influence of civilization in the Pacific has tended to increase rather than diminish all forms of clandestine sexual depravity.

I have heard competent and unprejudiced observers state that the Fijians were fully as affectionate in heathen times as at present. Family affection fortunately springs from nature itself and is not a product of our system of life, however cultured or barbarous. One sees the naked women of Australia, whose bodies are covered with self-inflicted scars, gaze rapturously upon their children and exhibit maternal love as truly as could any European mother, and even Wilkes, who refers to the Fijians as "the most barbarous and savage race now existing upon the globe," states that he saw "engaged couples walking affectionately arm-in-arm as with us."

One of the saddest, because the most apparent change that has affected the lives of the Pacific islanders is the needless decay of their arts. War, and the ceremonies and obligations of religion once provided the major motive for the maintenance and development of varied crafts. In fact, the intent of practically every piece of decorative work was either to propitiate the gods and tribal spirits, or to frighten a real or imaginary enemy. Nor is this peculiar to savage tribes, for all the complex ornaments which adorn the yokes of horses in Naples are "evil eye" charms which have come down almost unaltered from Roman times.

The missionary soon saw that most of his so-called converts had only added the white man's god to those of their ancestors. In order, therefore, to obliterate old beliefs, he discouraged the making of all "symbols of heathenism," and, as these were displayed in almost every implement, art fell at once under the awe-inspiring ban of his displeasure.

Yet the decline of native art was to some degree inevitable even if the missionaries had attempted to foster and preserve it, for it perished chiefly because of its inadaptability, and the absence of a market for its wares. The cheapest calico is softer and more enduring than the best of tapa, the coarsest canvas sail is superior to that woven of pandanus leaves, the beautiful adze of polished stone fails wholly when placed in competition with even the "trade hatchet."

Yet in each group there was at least some native art which, had it been cared for by the whites, might have been preserved so that in a more or less modified form it might have furnished a permanent and progressively important means of livelihood to the natives, and thus have become a means of maintaining their racial entity and self-respect.

Art was the highest expression of their intellectual life, an absorbing field for their ambition, a means of gratifying their instinct for the beautiful, and a record of their history and their conception of the universe. It meant far more to them than it does to us with our widely varied interests, and to this the European was blind when he permitted its destruction.

All over the south seas in proportion as white men have become dominant native arts have withered. Once the canoe was built of separate pieces skilfully calked and lashed together, and its outrigger was a marvel of flexibility and strength. Yet everywhere it degenerates into a crudely hollowed log, crossed by two rough sticks to which the outrigger is rigidly tied. The house, once shapely in form and carefully thatched, degenerates into a mere shack, and every carved bowl, paddle and implement becomes rude, ugly and misshapen. All care in manufacture degenerates, and in proportion does the light of their intellectual life fade out. A hopeless apathy, a listless lack of interest in all around them overcomes their dulled minds and their lives, like those of prisoners, are no longer worth the while of living, for hope cannot flower within the stifle of the cold gray walls of bigotry's bastile.

Pleasures and sports suffer as do the arts. The surf-board riders of Hawaii are now rarely seen, dances and songs are being constantly suppressed, and many happy things that once filled their minds with joy, and were beautiful in their eyes, have vanished never to be theirs again. But one resource is left to their idle minds, and clandestine immorality saps their strength. As the Government Commission in Fiji reports premature civilization, mental apathy and lack of ambition under the new conditions are among the most important causes of the decline of the population.

This carefully selected commission was appointed by the British government in Fiji to inquire into the causes of the decrease in the native population, and after long investigation the conclusions of the commissioners were published by the Colony in 1896. It is probable that in 1859 there were about 200,000 natives; in 1868, 170,000; in 1871, 140,000; in 1881 there were 114,700 and in 1891, 105,800 while in 1901 the population had still further declined to 94,400, and the males outnumbered the females in the proportion of 8 to 7. In 1911 there were but 87,096 natives, and if the decline continues at its present rate the last Fijian must die before another century has passed.

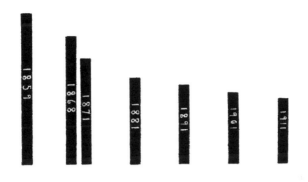

*ILLUSTRATING THE DECLINE IN THE NATIVE POPULATION OF THE FIJI ISLANDS FROM 1859 to 1911.*

The commission decides that children have ceased to be useful, and whereas in old days they strengthened the tribe in war, they now suffer neglect. The birth rate is higher than that of England yet only 11/20 of the children survive to be one year old. Another cause is said to be the general want of vitality due to the effects of past epidemics, such as the "wasting sickness" in 1797, the dysentery of 1803 and the measles of 1875. One is, however, inclined to believe that no permanent evil effects could be produced as a result of these physiological disasters. No matter how severe the epidemic, those who are physically the best are the most apt to survive and become the progenitors of successive generations, and thus the race might even be improved through natural selection. There is no evidence tending to prove that the black death of the fourteenth century or the plague in London in the time of Charles II. resulted in any permanent physical deterioration of the races they affected. The Fijians may be a vanishing people, but in physical appearance they remain superior as of old, and their superb stature and mental attainments appear not to have declined even though the race as a whole be dying.

There is, however, one cardinal evil in the Fijian situation and that is the severe strain of child-raising which falls upon the women in a country wherein the proper food for the maintenance of lactation has not yet been produced in sufficient quantity. The children, being thus in a peculiar sense dependent upon their mothers, will be profoundly affected by any conditions which produce injury to the women of the tribe.

Yaws, dysentery and whooping cough are now primary causes of the decline of population. Among minor causes the committee mentions the abolition of polygamy; for under monogamy the mother must not only tend her child, but gather the food and cultivate the soil, whereas in polygamous days these latter duties were taken over by the other wives during the early period of the infant's life.

The report makes it clear that the decline is due chiefly to the high death rate of children, and also that we must proceed very slowly and sympathetically, using as little force as possible, in the introduction of civilization. The old socialism must gradually be replaced by a certain measure of individualism, and the warrior's ambitions must give place to those of the craftsman. Hygiene as a subject of primary importance must be taught not only in the schools, but chiefly by example, upon the plan of the college settlement, by teachers living in so far as possible as the natives themselves now live, thus slowly changing the habits of life of those around them, and indeed these teachers should themselves *be natives* of the most enlightened type, and maintained in government employ.

A most interesting sociological experiment has been conducted by the British in their government of the Fijians. It is one of the very few instances wherein altruism is the key-note in the rule of the strong over the weak, and its maintenance through all these years in the face of much discouragement and expense is an honor to Great Britain, in the pride of which all the world may share—it is a rare triumph of idealism over selfishness.

As Mr. Allardyce, then colonial secretary, said to me:

We came here not as conquerors but through invitation, and the best we have to give is none too good for these people who have entrusted their destiny to our care.

Indeed, if the South Sea Islanders are now to be saved *new* interests and *new* arts must be developed by them, and new ambitions other than the withered remnants of the old must be created. Industrial schools are sadly needed in the Pacific, and the dawn of the first real progress will appear when men like Booker Washington arise among the natives of Fiji. The establishment of non-sectarian manual training schools such as his, in so far as possible under native teachers and supported by native efforts, might soon revolutionize their whole system of life, and change them from well-behaved captives into purposeful men and women.

The missionaries now conduct nearly all the schools in Fiji, and it is much to their credit that illiteracy is almost as rare as in Germany, all the present generation being able to read and write their own language. These schools are fundamentally good, but the natives should be taught not only how to pray, but also how to labor and to live. The missionaries would doubtless welcome an opportunity to extend the scope of native education, but the expense of establishing trade schools is too great for their resources and the project demands government aid. That the return to the state would ultimately far more than repay the outlay cannot be doubted, for even the non-altruistic Dutch well know the profit accruing to Java and hence to themselves through the establishment of agricultural schools for natives.

Every indication of an initiative among the Fijians in the direction of craft-development should be wisely encouraged instead of being, as at present, smothered under the cloak of a paternalism that obliterates error only by crushing endeavor.

It may be confidently hoped that the British government which has labored so persistently and at such constant expense to develop Fiji "for the Fijians" and not for the surfeit of those who would selfishly exploit the natives, will take this final step and render it possible for the natives to raise *themselves* to a position of self-dependence. This was, indeed, the confessed intention of certain high officials of the colony whom I enjoyed the pleasure of meeting when in Fiji. So consistent have the English been in their effort actually to civilize and elevate the Fijians that their policy has been pursued for years despite financial loss and the frequent protests of the whites, as is evidenced by the steady decline of the white population from

2,750 in 1871 to 2,036 in 1891, since which time it has slowly risen, becoming 3,707 in 1911. The public debt in 1910 was £104,115 and the native taxes amounted only to about £16,000, the principal source of revenue being derived from customs receipts which were £129,552, the latter being, of course, an indirect tax upon the colony itself.

Since 1874, settlers have been discouraged from employing Fijians upon their plantations, for the native population was rapidly being enslaved by the whites. In order to supply the necessary labor, Hindoo coolies from Calcutta were imported, but it seems unfortunate that these usually remained in Fiji after the expiration of their terms of service and there are now 40,300 in the group. They are a clannish, industrious, bigoted race whom the Fijians despise and with whom they do not mingle. Indeed, there are far more half-breds between the whites and Fijians than between Fijians and Hindoos.

Although all native arts have suffered and some have wholly disappeared in Fiji, the introduction of European methods has been slower in this group than elsewhere in the Pacific. Spears and clubs and other implements of war are no longer made unless, indeed, it be to sell to tourists, and the dancing masks and wigs of former days have disappeared, along with the cannibal forks. Once the natives took great pride in their war-clubs, and a man's rank was indicated by the fashion of his club and his manner of carrying it, only chiefs being permitted to bear it over the shoulder as we would a gun. The handle was notched whenever the club had served to kill a man, and such a weapon was called a "ngandro" to distinguish it from common clubs. Indeed the more famous clubs were given individual names, a certain chief being the proud possessor of one called "the giver of rest." Elaborately carved, and built up, spears of iron-wood ten or fifteen feet long were common, and were sometimes tipped with the spine of the sting-ray, which upon breaking within the wound caused certain death. In the distant villages among the mountains of the large islands, spears and clubs were still to be seen in the houses in 1899, but from more accessible places they have long since disappeared to crowd the shelves of our museums. Everywhere the natives of the coasts have yielded, and more or less conformed to the white man's customs, but only a few miles inland, isolated by the dense forests or walled in by mountains, they were in 1900 almost as in heathen times. Yet even in these remote places the natives are not wholly separated from the world, for news is carried rapidly by word of mouth, and Wilkes speaks of a case in which a message was transmitted 20 miles through a forested country in less than six hours.

The pursuit of war was once the chief concern of the Fijians, and was often conducted in a very ceremonious fashion. An offended chief thrust sticks into the ground and removed them only when appeased. If war was determined upon a herald was sent to the village of the enemy to announce the fact. As is universal with primitive people, the mustering of the army was the occasion for much extravagant boasting, and their faces were painted red or half red and half black. Miss Gordon Cumming gives a striking description of the wild wardance and the boasts of the warriors who assembled at the call of Sir Arthur Gordon to take part in the war against the cannibal tribes of the Singatoka River in the mountains. "This is only a musket" cried one warrior "but I carry it." By contrast the men from Mbau came up in stately fashion, their spokesman saying "This is Mbau, that is enough."

The towns were often fortified with wooden stockades or stone walls, and were sometimes surrounded by moats. There are no records of protracted sieges, for the attacking party never could carry sufficient food to enable them to remain long before the walls of the besieged. They depended almost wholly upon treachery, ambushes or sudden and unexpected assaults; and to kill a woman or a child or even a pig was considered a creditable feat, as when Thakombau's warriors returned to Mbau boasting, "We have killed seven of the enemy's pigs and two women." Before the introduction of firearms, it is probable that native warfare caused but little loss of life, for fear kept the combatants skulking at a fairly safe distance from one another.

Wilkes, who himself made war upon the natives of Malolo after they had killed Lieutenant Underwood and Midshipman Henry, describes their martial customs at great length and should be read by those interested in the matter.

The cruelties practised when a town was overcome were unspeakable, and on the island of Wakaia the chief and all within his village threw themselves over a high cliff to be dashed to death rather than surrender.

Fijian warfare, like that of cannibalism, is indeed a sordid subject. Not a single struggle waged by any tribe was for the establishment of a worthy principle. Lust for murder, the capture of women, revenge for real, or more often imaginary, insults were the actuating motives of all native wars. There is in the language no word expressing disapprobation for the killing of a human being. Indeed, no matter how brutal, treacherous or cowardly the murder of man, woman or child the murderer immediately gained the proud title of koroi, which insured to him a good position among the spirits of the world to come, and permitted him to blacken his face and chest with a peculiar warpaint. Murder was thus an open sesame to social distinction and religious well-being.

The Fijians are courageous in the sense that all men are brave when wrought up to the point of action, and when facing a situation they understand. Their first sight of a horse, however, drove even the doughtiest warriors to take refuge in the trees, and when upon a dark night Wilkes came to anchor off the coast and set off rockets, the silence of the shore broke into a long shriek of terror, village after village catching the contagion of the fright. Even to-day the white man inspires a mysterious lurking fear, and in the mountain villages and in parts rarely visited by Europeans, the women and little children shrink and run at your approach, and even the men seem somewhat "stage struck." To their minds we must be past masters of witchcraft.

Indeed, in common with all beliefs and practises which may be securely hidden from the eyes of

Europeans, witchcraft still survives in Fiji, as it does among the lower classes of Europe and America. The natives are fond of the "occult" and several miracles are still performed. Thus at the village of Nandawa, on Koro island, an old man stands upon a high rock and calls to the sea-turtles, shouting in Fijian, Come! Come! We are tired of waiting! upon which several turtles appear swimming toward the shore. It is highly probable that these are regularly fed and are thus always ready for the "miracle" when strangers visit the town. Koro, by the way, is the island to which the souls of all dead pigs were supposed to go to their valhalla.

At the village of Rukua on Mbenga a curious miracle play is enacted. Near the town there is a circular pit about twenty feet in diameter, the bottom of which is lined with brown-colored volcanic stones, a ring of large flat ones lying near the edge around the bottom of the depression. The pit is filled with dry sticks and a fire is maintained until the stones are red hot. Then the embers are brushed away, and out of the forest there comes a procession of young men gaily adorned with garlands of flowers and well polished with cocoanut oil. They chant as they tread slowly and deliberately over the hot stones, and then vanish into the woods, apparently uninjured; upon which pigs and vegetables are placed upon the stones and are covered with leaves and earth, and a thoroughly cooked feast is soon ready for both guests and performers. Professor Langley witnessed a similar exhibition in the Society Islands, and discovered that the radiation from the surface of the volcanic stones is very great, while the stones themselves are poor conductors of heat, thus the surface soon cools while enough heat still remains within to serve in cooking the feast. The natives cannot be induced to walk over limestone, which is a good conductor and poor radiator, the surface thus remaining hot. However, the great thickness of the skin upon the sole of their unshod feet accounts in some measure for their ability to perform this "miracle." In all respects natural sole leather is superior to that provided by the "leather trust."

A pleasing art which still survives, but is doomed to extinction, is the making and decorating of tapa, or *masi*, as it is called in Fiji, where it is still used for screens in houses, and for various decorative purposes. Women alone take part in the manufacture of tapa. They carefully cultivate the paper mulberry (*Broussonetia papyrifera*), and, when about six feet high, the young trees are cut down, and the bark peeled off and soaked in water.

The outer skin is then scraped off with a sharp-edged shell, and the soft fibrous inner bark is ready for beating, although it may be kept indefinitely before this process is begun. For beating, the strips of bark must be thoroughly water-soaked and soft, and two are placed one over the other upon a flattened log and beaten with a rectangular mallet, *iki*, having three of its flat sides grooved and one plane. Each pair of strips of an inch in original width may thus be beaten out into a thin sheet of felted fibers nine inches wide, although the length is reduced. Separate sheets are then welded together by beating, the overlapping edges being first glued with a paste made from arrowroot boiled in water, this welding being so cleverly done that it is almost impossible to tell where the pieces overlie one another. The sheet is then spread upon the grass and exposed to the sun to bleach. These sheets may be very large, one we measured being 160 feet long and 12 feet wide, but Williams mentions a sheet 180 yards long!

After being bleached, they produce a pattern upon the tapa with a brown dye derived from the *Aleurites triloba*, the dull color of which is relieved at intervals by large black circular spots, thus by contrast giving a bright and effective pattern. This process of decorating is described in detail by

Thomas Williams in his most interesting work upon "Fiji and the Fijians." Strips of bamboo are placed in the form of the design upon a flat surface, or the design is carved in relief in a board. Then the tapa is stretched over the template and the cloth rubbed with the dye, whereupon the color adheres to all raised places and fails to appear in the hollows, and a "printed" pattern is produced. So characteristic are the checquered patterns of the tapas of the several islands that the locality of each piece can be determined upon the most casual inspection. The black and white tapas of Taviuni are most effective, and those of Lakemba probably the most artistic made in the group. It seems strange that although these tapas have for ages been printed in designs, little or no meaning was associated with the details of the pattern. There were, however, certain appropriate patterns for weddings and other ceremonies, and the flags of the various classes of warriors were more or less distinctive. Thus at Rewa the banner of the king's or high chief's party was white with four or five vertical black stripes at one end, that of the vunivalu or general had horizontal stripes, and that of the land owners was plain white. Yet the tapa flags never became tribal emblems, on the one hand, or personal coats-of-arms, on the other, but remained merely class badges, and thus no precise symbolism was associated with the designs.

In groups other than Fiji the inner bark of the bread-fruit tree, and of the yellow hibiscus *Paritium tiliaceum* are used in making tapa. Yellow turmeric, bone charcoal, brilliant red and rich brown dyes, are displayed upon tapas of the Pacific.

The art must surely disappear, for Manchester is now printing calicos in the patterns of the native tapas and these are being sold to the islanders, who prefer them to designs of their own making. In some groups traders have brought in anilin dyes which the natives call "missionary colors," the word "missionary" being applied to almost any newly introduced thing. Thus is an ancient and primitive art being debased, and another means of employment must disappear from native life. At the time of the author's visits the beating of the *ikis*(mallets) was the most characteristic sound in a Fijian village, but in a few more years this too must go the way of many another activity which once engrossed the attention and stimulated the imagination of the natives.

Tapa in Fiji was once used for the white turbans of the chiefs and the simple waist band or *malo* worn by all men. In the case of chiefs the ends of the waist cloth formed long streamers, those of king

Tanoa being so long that they trailed upon the ground. When yaqona was served, all chiefs removed their turbans, excepting only the Roko Tui of Mbau who was regarded as being a human personification of a god.

The women never wore tapa, but were clothed in the simple *liku* or waist band of hibiscus bark or grasses which is still worn among the mountain tribes, although along the coast the Europeans have abolished both it and the *malo*, obliging all to wear a waist-cloth of calico. In some respects they were a modest people before these changes were effected, and fortunately for the natives their new rulers did not oblige them to don more clothing. In other parts of the Pacific the missionaries have forced the natives to wear European garments, far too hot for tropical climates. Such clothes are so expensive that few or none of the natives can afford to own more than one suit, and this soon becomes a filthy menace to health. Tuberculosis stalks in when European clothes appear, and all unprejudiced observers will agree that the most diseased and immoral races now in the Pacific are those who have been obliged to wear the most clothing.

Their own clothes permitted the natives to bathe freely, but the whites now demand that the natives shall don special bathing suits or at least enter the water clothed in some European garments. This practically forces them either to abstain from their health-giving sport of former times or to swim fully clothed, as they now do in Hawaii. These cold wet clothes are a cause of influenza leading to tuberculosis, and everywhere the natives are less cleanly as Christians than they were as heathens.

In former times the Fijians took great pride in the arrangement of their hair, and a wide range of individual taste was permitted in this respect, as may be seen in the illustrations given by Williams in his "Fiji and the Fijians," or the colored plate published in the narrative of the voyage of the *Challenger*. Usually they trained the hair to grow into a huge thick mop standing out on all sides fully eight inches from the head, and sometimes as much as 62 inches in circumference. In order to effect this, the hair was saturated with oil mixed with charcoal and then dyed so that blue, white, brilliant red, black or parti-colored mops were in fashion. The high chiefs had barbers whose sole duty was to care for the hair of their masters, and whose hands were tabu from feeding themselves so that others had to provide them with food and drink. Such a barber might not remove a cigarette from his mouth or hold it in his hands and was thus obliged to twist a twig around it in order to avoid the weed's coming in contact with his hands. Curiously enough, barbers might work in their gardens, but were not permitted to use their hands in eating their own vegetables. Probably no savage race devoted more care to hair and beards than did the Fijians. They are very rarely bald, and indeed this was considered to be a great disfigurement, and the defect was concealed by a wig. To preserve these unwieldy mops of hair, the natives were obliged to sleep upon a wooden pillow which was placed under the neck and held the head four or five inches above the floor.

To the European, all customs are apt to be classed as "bad" in proportion as they *differ* from those of his own race, but it should be said that in Fiji the missionaries have been more conservative and displayed far more sympathy and sense in their reforms than elsewhere in the Pacific. Nevertheless, all forms of really active exercises or keen enjoyment have a somewhat wicked appearance to a certain type of religious mind, and unhappily the mediocre man is the one who is apt to rule in deciding the fate of such affairs. They too often fail to see that when an old custom is to be abolished something should be devised to take its place. Thus their vandalism of bigotry has resulted in destroying or hindering the open practise of nearly all the old arts and amusements; and almost nothing but hymns and prayers and a cheerless sabbath resembling that of Puritan days in old New England have been given to the natives in exchange for all they have been forced to surrender.

The Fijians once took great delight in their club dances, but these have now been repressed and have lost much of their former animation. In one of these festivities which we witnessed the men leaped frantically in perfect unison, branishing their clubs and throwing them from hand to hand, often shielding their eyes with one hand as if searching for a hidden or distant enemy. At regular intervals they shouted *Wa hoo!* in a fierce yell that could have been heard at a distance of a quarter of a mile, while all the village crowded in a square around the dancers, beating log drums, clapping hands and chanting something which sounded like "Somo seri rangi tu Somo seri somo," over and over again. Often the meanings of words used in their songs are unknown to the natives of modern times. Wilkes gives an excellent description of a club-dance in which the best dancers were mimicked by a clown covered from head to foot with green and dried leaves, and wearing a mask half orange and half black.

The milder mekes (songs with gestures) are wisely encouraged by the missionaries, and these are still a source of constant amusement to the natives. Fiji has not yet been suppressed into a realm of sullen silence as have too many parts of the Pacific.

There is a fascination in the elemental force of the word-pictures in these songs. We stifle in the heavy air of the dull and ominous calm. Then comes the rising roar of the onrush and our hearts go out to the frail canoes struggling so bravely in a maddened sea, and the pathos of life and death is there when the hot sun glares down once more, and the ripples glint unheedingly around the silent floating thing over which the sea-birds scream.

## Part IV

The Fijians had a well-organized social system with six classes of society: 1) Kings and queens (*Tuis and Andis*). 2) Chiefs of districts (*Rokos*). 3) Chiefs of villages, priests (*Betes*), and land owners (*Mata-ni-vanuas*). 4) Distinguished warriors of low birth, chiefs of the carpenter caste (*Rokolas*), and chiefs of the turtle fishermen. 5) Common people (*Kai-si*). 6) Slaves taken in battle.

The high chiefs still inspire great respect, and indeed it has been the policy of the British government to maintain a large measure of their former authority. Thus of the 17 provinces into which the group was divided, 11 are governed by high chiefs entitled *Roko Tui*, and there are about 176 inferior chiefs who are the head men of districts, and 31 native magistrates. In so far as may be consistent with order and civilization these chiefs are permitted to govern in the old paternal manner, and they are veritably patriarchs of their people. The district chiefs are still elected by the land owners, mata-ni-vanuas, by a showing of hands as of old.

Independent of respect paid to those in authority, rank is still reverenced in Fiji. Once acting under the kind permission and advice of our generous friend Mr. Allardyce, the colonial secretary, and accompanied by my ship-mates Drs. Charles H. Townsend, and H. F. Moore, I went upon a journey of some days into the interior of Viti Levu, our guide and companion being Ratu Pope Seniloli, a grandson of king Thakombau, and one of the high chiefs of Mbau. Upon meeting Ratu Pope every native dropped his burdens, stepped to the side of the wood-path and crouched down, softly chanting the words of the tame, muduo! wo! No one ever stepped upon his shadow, and if desirous of crossing his path they passed in front, never behind him. Clubs were lowered in his presence, and no man stood fully erect when he was near. The very language addressed to high chiefs is different from that used in conversation between ordinary men, these customs being such that the inferior places himself in a defenceless position with respect to his superior.

It is a chief's privilege to demand service from his subjects; which was fortunate for us, for when we started down the Waidina River from Nabukaluka our canoes were so small and overloaded that the ripples were constantly lapping in over the gunwale, threatening momentarily to swamp us. Soon, however, we came upon a party of natives in a fine large canoe, and after receiving their tama Ratu Pope demanded: "Where are you going"? The men, who seemed somewhat awestricken, answered that it had been their intention to travel up the river. Whereupon Ratu Pope told them that this they might do, but we would take their canoe and permit them to continue in ours. To this they acceded with the utmost cheerfulness, although our noble guide would neither heed our protests nor permit us to reward them for their service, saying simply, "I am a chief. You may if you choose pay me." In this manner we continued to improve our situation by "exchanging" with every canoe we met which happened to be better than our own, until finally our princely friend ordered a gay party of merry-makers out of a fine large skiff, which they cheerfully "exchanged" for our leaky canoes and departed singing happily, feeling honored indeed that this opportunity had come to them to serve the great chief Ratu Pope Seniloli; and thus suffering qualms of conscience, we sailed to our destination leaving a wake of confusion behind us. Moreover I forgot to mention that many natives had by Ratu Pope's orders been diverted from their intended paths and sent forward to announce the coming of himself and the "American chiefs." Thus does one of the Royal house of Mbau proceed through Fiji.

At first sight such behavior must appear autocratic, to say the least, but it should be remembered that a high chief has it in his power fully to recompense those about him, and this without the payment of a penny. Indeed, many intelligent natives still regret the introduction of money into their land, saying that all the white man's selfishness had been developed through its omnipotence. In Fiji to-day there are no poor, for such would be fed and given a house by those who lived beside them. The white man's callous brutality in ignoring the appeal of misery is incomprehensible to the natives of Fiji. "Progress" they have not in the sense that one man possesses vast wealth and many around him struggle helplessly, doomed to life-long poverty; nor have they ambition to toil beyond that occasional employment required to satisfy immediate wants. Yet if life be happy in proportion as the summation of its moments be contented, the Fijians are far happier than we. Old men and women rest beneath the shade of cocoa-palms and sing with the youths and maidens, and the care-worn faces and bent bodies of "civilization" are still unknown in Fiji.

They still have something we have lost and never can regain.

It is impossible to draw a line between personal service such as was rendered to Ratu Pope and a regular tax (lala) for the benefit of the entire community or the support of the communal government; and the recognition of this fact actuated the English to preserve much of the old system and to command the payment of taxes in produce, rather than in money.

Land tenure in Fiji is a subject so complex that heavy volumes might be written upon it. In general it may be said that the chief can sell no land without the consent of his tribe. Cultivated land belonged to the man who originally farmed it, and is passed undivided to all his heirs. Waste land is held in common. Native settlers who have been taken into the tribes from time to time have been permitted to farm some of the waste land, and for this privilege they and their heirs must pay a yearly tribute to the chief either in produce or in service. Thus this form of personal lala is simply rent. The whole subject of land-ownership has given the poor English a world of trouble, as one may see who cares to read the official reports of the numerous intricate cases that have come before the courts.

For example, one party based their claims to land on the historic fact that their ancestors had eaten the chief of the original owners, and the solemn British court allowed the claim.

Basil Thomson in his interesting work upon "The Fijians; a Study of the Decline of Custom," has given an authoritative summary of the present status of taxation and land tenure, land being registered under a modification of the Australian Torrens system.

In order to protect these child-like people from the avarice of our own race they are not permitted to sell their lands, and the greater portion of the area of Fiji is still held by the natives. The Hawaiian Islands now under our own rule furnish a sad contrast, for here the natives are reduced by poverty to a degraded state but little above that of peonage. The Fijians. on the other hand, may not sell, but may with the consent of the commissioner of native affairs lease their lands for a period of not more than twenty years.

The Fijians appear never to have been wholly without a medium of exchange, for sperm-whale's teeth have always had a recognized purchasing power, but are more especially regarded as a means of expressing good will and honesty of purpose. A whale's tooth is as effective to secure compliance with the terms of a bargain as an elaborately engraved bond would be with us. More commonly, however, exchanges are direct, each man bringing to the village green his taro, yaqona, yams or fish and exchanging with his neighbors; the rare disputes being settled by the village chief.

In traveling you will discover no hotels, but will be entertained in the stranger's houses, and in return for your host's hospitality you should make presents to the chief. Indeed to journey in good fashion you should be accompanied by a train of bearers carrying heavy bags full of purposed gifts, and nowhere in the world is the "rate per mile" higher than in Polynesia.

As in all communities, including our own world of finance, a man's wealth consists not only in what he possesses but even more so in the number of people from whom he can beg or borrow. Wilkes records an interesting example of this, for he found that the rifle and other costly presents he had presented to King Tanoa were being seized upon by his (Tanoa's) nephew who as his vasu had a right to take whatever he might select from the king's possessions. Indeed, in order to keep his property in sight, Tanoa was forced to give it to his own sons, thus escaping the rapacity of his nephew. The construction of the British law is such that a vasu who thus appropriates property to himself could be sued and forced to restore it, but not a single Fijian has yet been so mean as to bring such a matter into court.

An individual as such can hardly be said to own property, for nearly all things belong to his family or clan, and are shared among cousins. This condition is responsible for that absence of personal ambition and that fatal contentment with existing conditions, which strikes the white man as so illogical, but which is nevertheless the dominant feature of the social fabric of the Polynesians, and which has hitherto prevented the introduction of "ideals of modern progress." The natives are happy; why work when every reasonable want is already supplied? None are rich in material things, but none are beggars excepting in the sense that all are such. No one can be a miser, a capitalist, a banker, or a "promoter" in such a community, and thieves are almost unknown. Indeed, the honesty of the Fijians is one of those virtues which has excited the comment of travelers. Wilkes, who loathed them as "condor-eyed savages," admits that the only thing which any native attempted to steal from the Peacock was a hatchet, and upon being detected the chief requested the privilege of taking the man ashore in order that he might be roasted and eaten.

Theft was always severely punished by the chief; Maafu beating a thief with the stout stalk of a cocoanut leaf until the culprit's life was despaired of, and Tui Thakau wrapping one in a tightly wound rope so that not a muscle could move while the wretch remained exposed for an entire day to the heat of the sun.

During Professor Alexander Agassiz's cruises in which he visited nearly every island of the Fijis, and the natives came on board by hundreds, not a single object was stolen, although things almost priceless in native estimation lay loosely upon the deck. Once, indeed, when the deck was deserted by both officers and crew and fully a hundred natives were on board, we found a man who had been gazing wistfully for half an hour at a bottle which lay upon the laboratory table. Somehow he had managed to acquire a shilling, a large coin in Fiji, and this he offered in exchange for the coveted bottle. One can never forget his shout of joy and the radiance of his honest face as he leaped into his canoe after having received it as a gift.

Even the great chief Ratu Epele of Mbau beamed with joy when presented with a screw-capped glass tobacco jar, and Tui Thakau of Somo somo had a veritable weakness for bottles and possessed a large collection of these treasures.

Intelligent and well-educated natives who know whereof they speak have told me that they desire not the white man's system, entailing as it does untold privation and heart-burnings to the many that the few may enjoy a surfeit of mere material things. As the natives say, "The white man possesses more than we, but his life is full of toil and sorrow, while our days are happy as they pass."

Thus in the Pacific life is of today; the past is dead, and the future when it comes will pass as today is passing. Life is a dream, an evanescent thing, all but meaningless, and real only as is the murmur of the surf when the sea-breeze comes in the morning, and man awakens from the oblivion of night.

Hoarded wealth inspires no respect in the Pacific, and indeed, were it discovered, its possession would justify immediate confiscation. Yet man must raise idols to satisfy his instinct to worship things above his acquisition, and thus rank is the more reverenced because respect for property is low. Even today there is something god-like in the presence of the high chiefs, and none will cross the shadow of the king's house. Even in war did a common man kill a chief he himself was killed by men of his own tribe.

As it is with property so with relationships. The family ties seem loosened; every child has two sets of parents, the adopted and the real, and relationships founded upon adoption are more respected than the real. Rank descends mainly through the mother. The son of a high chief by a common woman is a low chief, or even a commoner, but the son of a chieftainess by a common man is a chief. Curiously, there are no words in Fijian which are the exact equivalent of widow and widower. In the Marshall group the chief is actually the husband of all the women of his tribe, and as Lorimer Fison has said in his "Tales from Old Fiji," their designation and understanding of relationships suggests that there was once a time when "all the women were the wives of every man, and all the men were the husbands of every woman," as indeed was almost the case in Tahiti at the time of Captain Cook's visit to this island.

The social customs of Fiji are rarely peculiar to Fiji itself, but commonly show their relationship or identity with those of the Polynesians or Papuans. Curiously indeed, while the original stock of the Fijians was probably pure Papuan, their social and economic systems are now dominated by Polynesian ideas, and only among the mountain tribes do we find a clear expression of the crude Papuan systems of life and thought. This in itself shows that under stimulation the Fijians are capable of advancement in cultural ideals.

This superposition of a Polynesian admixture upon a barbarous negroid stock may account for the anomalous character of the Fijians, for in the arts they equalled or in some things excelled the other island peoples of the Pacific, and some of their customs approached closely to the cultural level of the Polynesians, but in certain fundamental things they remained the most fiendish savages upon earth. Indeed we should expect that contact with a somewhat high culture would introduce new wants, and thus affect their arts more profoundly than their customs.

In common with all primitive peoples, their names of men and women are descriptive of some peculiarity or circumstance associated with the person named. Indeed, names were often changed after important events in a person's life, thus our old friend Thakombau began life as Seru, then after the coup d'etat in which he slaughtered his father's enemies and reestablished Tanoa's rule in Mbau he was called Thakombau (evil to Mbau). At the time he also received another name Thikinovu (centipede) in allusion to his stealthiness in approaching to bite his enemy, but this designation, together with his "missionary" name "Ebenezer," did not survive the test of usage. Miss Gordon Cumming gives an interesting list of Fijian names translated into English. For women they were such as Spray of the Coral Reef, Queen of Parrot's Land, Queen of Strangers, Smooth Water, Wife of the Morning Star, Mother of Her Grandchildren, Ten Whale's Teeth, Mother of Cockroaches, Lady Nettle, Drinker of Blood, Waited For, Rose of Rewa, Lady Thakombau, Lady Flag, etc. The men's names were such as The Stone (eternal) God, Great Shark, Bad Earth, Bad Stranger, New Child, More Dead Man's Flesh, Abode of Treachery, Not Quite Cooked, Die Out of Doors, Empty Fire, Fire in the Bush, Eats Like a God, King of Gluttony, Ill Cooked, Dead Man, Revenge, etc.

In the religion of a people we have the most reliable clue to the history of their progress in culture and intelligence, for religions even when unwritten are potent to conserve old conceptions, and thus their followers advance beyond them, as does the intelligence of the twentieth century look pityingly upon the conception of the cruel and jealous God of the Old Testament, whose praises are nevertheless still sung in every Christian church. Thus in Tahiti the people were not cannibals, but the gods still appeared in the forms of birds that fed upon the bodies of the sacrificed. The eye of the victim was, indeed, offered to the chief, who raised it to his lips but did not eat it. In Samoa also where the practice of cannabalism was very rare and indulged in only under great provocation, some of the gods remained cannibals, and the surest way of appeasing any god was to be laid upon the stones of a cold oven. In Tahiti and Samoa, while most of the gods were malevolent, a few were kindly disposed towards mortals; in Fiji, however, they were all dreaded as the most powerful, sordid, cruel and vicious cannibal ghosts that have ever been conjured into being in the realm of thought.

All over the Pacific from New Zealand to Japan, and from New Guinea to Hawaii, ancestor-worship forms the backbone of every religion as clearly as it did in Greece or Rome. There are everywhere one or more very ancient gods who may always have existed and from whom all others are descended. Next in order of reverence, although not always in power, come their children, and finally the much more numerous grandchildren and remote descendants of these oldest and highest gods. Finally, after many generations, men of chieftain's rank were born to the gods. Thus a common man could never attain the rank of a high chief, for such were the descendants of the gods, while commoners were created out of other clay and designed to be servants to the chiefs.

But the process of god-making did not end with the appearance of men, for great chiefs and warriors after death became kalou yalo, or spirits, and often remained upon earth a menace to the unwary who might offend them. Curiously, these deified mortals might suffer a second death which would result in their utter annihilation, and while in Fiji we heard a tale of an old chief who had met with the ghost of his dead enemy and had killed him for the second and last time; the club which served in this miraculous victory having been hung up in the Mbure as an object of veneration.

Of a still lower order were the ghosts of common men or of animals, and most dreaded of all was the vengeful spirit of the man who had been devoured. The ghosts of savage Fiji appear all to have been malevolent and fearful beings, whereas those of the more cultured Polynesians were some of them benevolent. As Ellis says of the Tahitian mythology:

Each lovely island was made a sort of fairyland and the spells of enchantment were thrown over its varied scenes. The sentiment of the poet that

"Millions of spiritual creatures walk the earth, Unseen, both when we wake, and when we sleep"

was one familiar to their minds, and it is impossible not to feel interested in a people who were accustomed to consider themselves surrounded by invisible intelligences, and who recognized in the rising sun, the mild and silver moon, the shooting star, the meteor's transient flame, the ocean's roar, the tempest's blast, or the evening breeze the movements of mighty spirits.

The gods and ghosts of Fiji often entered into the bodies of animals or men, especially idiots.

Thus when the Carnegie Institution Expedition arrived at the Murray Islands in Torres Straits, the scientific staff were much pleased at the decided evidences of respect shown by the natives until it came out that the Islanders considered their white guests to be semi-idiots, and hence powerful sorcerers to be placated. Fijian religion had developed into the oracular stage, and the priest after receiving prayers and offerings would on occasions be entered into by the god. Tremors would overspread his body, the flesh of which would creep horribly. His veins would swell, his eyeballs protrude with excitement and his voice, becoming quavering and unnatural, would whine out strange words, words spoken by the god himself and unknown to the priest who as his unconscious agent was overcome by violent convulsions. Slowly the contortions grew less and with a start the priest would awaken, dash his club upon the ground and the god would leave him. It may well be imagined that the priests were the most powerful agents of the chiefs in forwarding the interests of their masters, for, as in ancient Greece or Rome, nothing of importance was undertaken without first consulting the oracle.

Surrounded by multitudes of demons, ghosts, and genii who were personified in everything about him, religion was the most powerful factor in controlling Fijian life and politics. In fact, it entered deeply into every act the native performed. The gods were more monstrous in every way than man, but in all attributes only the exaggerated counterparts of Fijian chiefs.

War was constantly occurring among these gods and spirits, and even high gods could die by accident or be killed by those of equal rank so that at least one god, Samu, was thus dropped out of the mythology in 1847.

Ndengei was the oldest and greatest, but not the most universally reverenced god. He lived in a cavern in the northeastern end of Viti Levu, and usually appeared as a snake, or as a snake's head with a body of stone symbolizing eternal life. Among the sons and grandsons of Ndengei were Roko Mbati-ndua, the one-toothed lord; a fiend with a huge tooth projecting from his lower jaw and curving over the top of his head. He had bat's wings armed with claws and was usually regarded as a harbinger of pestilence. The mechanic's god was eight-handed, gluttony had eighty stomachs, wisdom possessed eight eyes. Other gods were the adulterer, the abductor of women of rank and beauty, the rioter, the brain-eater, the killer of men, the slaughter god, the god of leprosy, the giant, the spitter of miracles, the gods of fishermen and of carpenters, etc. One god hated mosquitoes and drove them away from the place where he lived. The names and stations of the gods are described by Thomas Williams, who has given the most detailed account of the old religion.

As with all peoples whose religion is barbarous, there were ways of obtaining sanctuary and many a man has saved his life by taking advantage of the tabus which secured their operation. No matter how desirous your host might be of murdering you, as long as you remained a guest under his roof you were safe, although were you only a few yards away from his door he would eagerly attack you.

But not only did the Fijians live in a world peopled by witches, wizards, prophets, seers and fortune-tellers, but there was a perfect army of fairies which overran the whole land, and the myths concerning which would have filled volumes could they ever have been gathered. The gnome-like spirits of the mountains had peaked heads, and were of a vicious, impish disposition, but were powerless to injure anyone who carried a fern leaf in his hand.

Sacred relics such as famous clubs, stones possessing miraculous powers, etc., were sometimes kept in Fijian temples, but there were no idols such as were prayed to by the Polynesians.

The fearful alternatives of heaven and hell were unknown to the Fijians. They believed in an eternal existence for men, animals, and even canoes and other inanimate things, but the future life held forth no prospect either of reward for virtues or punishment for evil acts committed while alive. So certain were they of a future life that they always referred to the dead as "the absent ones," and their land of shades (Mbulu) was not essentially different from the world they lived in. Indeed, their chief idea of death was that of rest, for as William's states, they have an adage: "Death is easy: Of what use is life? To die is rest."

There were, however, certain precautions the Fijian felt it advisable to take before entering the world to come. If he had been so unfortunate as not to have killed a man, woman or child, his duty would be the dismal one of pounding filth throughout eternity, and disgraceful careers awaited those whose ears were not bored or women who were not tatooed upon parts covered by the liku. Moreover, should a wife not accompany him (be strangled at the time of his death) his condition would be the dismal one of a spirit without a cook. Thirdly, as one was at the time of death so would the spirit be in the next world. It was therefore an advantage to die young, and people often preferred to be buried alive, or strangled, than to survive into old age. Lastly and most important, one must not die a bachelor, for such are invariably dashed to pieces by Nangganangga, even if they should succeed in eluding the grasp of the Great Woman, Lewa-levu, who flaunts the path of the departed spirits and searches for the ghosts of good-looking men. Let us imagine, however, that our shade departs this life in the best of form, young, married, with the lobes of his ears pierced, not dangerously handsome and a slayer of at least one human being. He starts upon the long journey to the Valhalla of Fiji. Soon he comes to a spiritual Pandanus at which he must throw the ghost of the whale's tooth which was placed in his hand at time of burial. If he succeeds in hitting the Pandanus, he may then wait until the spirit of his strangled wife comes to join him, after which he boards the canoe of the Fijian Charon and proceeds to Nambanggatai, where until 1847 there dwelt the god Samu, and after his death Samuyalo "the killer of souls."

This god remains in ambush in some spiritual mangrove bushes and thrusts a reed within the ground upon the path of the ghost as a warning not to pass the spot. Should the ghost be brave he raises his club in defiance, whereupon Samuyalo appears, club in hand, and gives battle. If killed in this combat, the ghost is cooked and eaten by the soul killer, and if wounded he must wander forever among the mountains, but if the ghost be victorious over the god he may pass on to be questioned by Ndengei, who may consign him either to Mburotu, the highest heaven, or drop him over a precipice into a somewhat inferior but still tolerable abode, Murimuria. This Ndengei does in accordance with the caprice of the moment and without reference either to the virtues or the faults of the deceased. Thus of those who die only a few can enter the higher heaven for the Great Woman and the Soul destroyer overcome the greater number of those who dare to face them. As for the victims of cannibal feasts, their souls are devoured by the gods when their bodies are eaten by man.

In temperament and ambitions the spirits of the dead remained as they were upon earth, but of more monstrous growth in all respects, resembling giants greater and more vicious than man. War and cannibalism still prevailed in heaven, and the character of the inhabitants seems to have been fiendish or contemptible as on earth; for the spirits of women who were not tattooed were unceasingly pursued by their more fortunate sisters, who tore their bodies with sharp shells, often making mincemeat of them for the gods to eat. Also the shade of any one whose ears had not been pierced was condemned to carry a masi log over his shoulder and submit to the eternal ridicule of his fellow spirits.

Altogether, this religion seems to have been as sordid, brutal and vicious as was the ancestral negroid stock of the Fijians. Connected with it there was, however, a rude mythology, clumsy but romantic, too much of which has been lost; for the natives of to-day have largely forgotten its stories or are ashamed to repeat it to the whites. In recent times the natives have tended to make their folk-lore conform to Biblical stories, or to adapt them to conditions of the present day. The interesting subject of the lingering influence of old beliefs upon the life of the natives of to-day has engaged the attention of Basil Thomson in "The Fijians, a Study of the Decay of Custom."

As in every British colony, the people are taught to respect the law. Sentences of imprisonment are meted out to natives for personal offences which if committed by white men would be punished by small fines, but the reason for this is that in the old native days such acts were avenged by murder, and it is to prevent crime that a prison term has been ordained. The natives take their imprisonment precisely as boys in boarding school regard a flogging, the victim commonly becoming quite a hero and losing no caste among his fellows. Indeed it is a common sight to see bands of from four to eight stalwart "convicts" a mile or more from the prison marching unguarded through the woods as they sing merrily on their way "home" to the jail. Once I recall seeing two hundred prisoners, all armed with long knives, engaged in cutting weeds along the roadside, chanting happily as they slashed, while a solitary native dressed only in a waist-cloth and armed only with a club stood guard at one end of the line, and this not near the prison, but in a lonely wood fully a mile from the nearest house.

In 1874, the British undertook the unique task of civilizing without exploiting a barbarous and degraded race which was drifting hopelessly into ruin. They began the solution of this complex problem by arresting the entire race and immuring them within the protecting walls of a system which recognized as its cardinal principle that the natives were unfit to think or act for themselves. For a generation the Fijians have been in a prison wherein they have become the happiest and best behaved captives upon earth. During this time they have become reconciled to a life of peace, and have forgotten the taste of human flesh; and while they cherish no love for the white man, they feel the might of his law and know that his decrees are as finalities of fate. All are serving life sentences to the white man's will, and the fire of their old ambition has cooled into the dull embers of resignation and then died into the apathy of contentment with things that are. Worse still, they have grown fond of their prison world, and the most pessimistic feature in the Fijian situation of to-day is the evident fact that there is almost no discontent among the natives. Old things have withered and decayed, but new ambition has not been born.

It is in no spirit of criticism of British policy that I have written the above paragraph for it was absolutely necessary that the race should "calm down" for a generation at least before it could be trusted to arise. Now, however, there are no more old chiefs whose memories hark back to days of savagery, and now for the first and only time has come the critical period in the unique governmental experiment the British have undertaken to perform, for now is the time when the child must learn to walk alone and the support of guardian arms must in kindness be withdrawn, else there must be nurtured but a cripple, not a man.

Among the generation of to-day the light of a new ambition must appear in Fiji or the race shall dwindle to its death. No real progress has been made by the Fijians; they have received much from their teachers, but have given nothing in return. They are in the position of a youth whose schooling has just been finished, life and action lie before him; will he awaken to his responsibility, develop his latent talent, character and power, and recompense his teachers by achievement, or will he sink into the apathy of a vile content?

The situation in Fiji is one of peculiar delicacy for the desire for better things must arise among the Fijians themselves, and should it once appear, the paternalism of the present government must be wisely withdrawn to permit of more and more freedom in proportion as the natives may become competent to think and act rightly for themselves. A cardinal difficulty is the unfortunate fact that the natives DESIRE no change, and even if individually discontented and ambitious, they know of no profession, arts or trades to which they might turn with hope of fortune. The establishment of manual training schools wherein money-making trades should be taught, if possible BY NATIVE teachers, is sorely needed in Fiji.

At present there is too little freedom of thought in Fiji; fear of the chief and of Samuyalo's club has been replaced by fear of the European and his hell. Free, fearless thought is the father of high action, and while their minds remain steeped in an apathy of dread there can be no soil in which the seed of independence can germinate.

Yet it is still possible that the Fijians may attain civilization. Of all the archipelagoes of Polynesia, Fiji alone may still be called the "Isles of Hope." As one who has known and grown to love these honest, hospitable, simple people, I can only hope that the day is not far distant when a leader may arise among them who will turn their faces toward the light of a brighter sky, and their hands to a worthier task than has ever yet been performed in Polynesia.

Yet why civilize them? Often does one ask oneself this question, but the answer comes as the voice of fate, "they must attain civilization or they must die." Should the population continue to decline at its present rate, the time is imminent when the dark-skinned men of Fiji will be not the natives, but the swarming progeny of the coolies of Calcutta.

Nowhere over all the wide Pacific have the natives been more wisely or unselfishly ruled than in Fiji, yet even here native life seems to be growing less and less purposeful year by year. In time it is hoped a reaction may set in and that with the decline of communism new ambitions may replace the old, but then will come the problem of the rich and the poor--a thing unknown in Fijian life to-day.

Hardly the first lessons in civilization have been taught in Polynesia, yet who can predict the noon day, should even the faintest glow appear in native hope. In former ages the Japanese were a barbarous insular people, and as in our own civilization the traditions and habits of rude Aryan ancestors still color our fundamental thoughts so in Japan we find evidences of a culture essentially similar to that of the Pacific Islands of to-day. The ancient ancestor worship of Japan is strangely like that of the tropical Pacific with its gods, the ghosts of long departed chiefs, and its high chief a living god to-day. Moreover in the Pacific Islands the house consists of but a single room, and such to-day is essentially the case in Japan, save only that delicate paper screens divide its originally unitary floor-space into temporary compartments. As in the South Seas, matting still covers the floor of the Japanese house, its roof is thatched, and is constructed before the sides are made, there is no chimney, the fire-place is an earthen space upon the floor or is sustained within an artistically molded bronze brazier, the refined descendant of the cruder hearth. In Polynesia as in Japan one seats oneself anywhere in tailor-fashion upon the floor, and upon this floor the meals are served, and here one sleeps at night, nor will the women partake of food in the presence of the men. In essential fundamental things of life the Japanese show their kinship in custom and tradition to the insular peoples of Asiatic origin now occupying the Pacific, and if Japan has attained to so great a height in culture and civilization, why may we not hope for better days for the South Sea Islanders?

Made in the USA
San Bernardino, CA
27 October 2017